Teaching Learning Strategies to Adolescents and Adults with Learning Disabilities

Teaching Learning Strategies to Adolescents and Adults with Learning Disabilities

B. Keith Lenz

Edwin S. Ellis

David Scanlon

8700 Shoal Creek Boulevard
Austin, Texas 78757

© 1996 by PRO-ED, Inc.
8700 Shoal Creek Boulevard
Austin, Texas 78757-6897

Library of Congress Cataloging-in-Publication Data

Lenz, B. Keith.
    Teaching learning strategies to adolescents and adults with
learning disabilities / B. Keith Lenz, Edwin Ellis, David Scanlon.
        p.   cm.
    ISBN 0-89079-650-5
    1. Learning disabled youth—Education—United States.
2. Learning, Psychology of—United States.   3. Cognitive styles in
children—United States.   4. Learning disabled youth—Behavior
modification—United States.   I. Ellis, Edwin.   II. Scanlon, David.
III. Title.
LC4705.L46   1995
371.9—dc20   94-41597
                                                            CIP

This book is designed in Fenice and Goudy.

Production Manager: Alan Grimes
Production Coordinator: Karen Swain
Art Director: Thomas Barkley
Reprints Buyer: Alicia Woods
Editor: Teri C. Sperry
Editorial Assistant: Claudette Landry

Printed in the United States of America

    4   5   6   7   8   9   10   05 04 03 02 01

Contents

Preface

Individuals with learning disabilities (LD) and others at risk need to learn the same things that other students learn. To do this successfully, they have a particular need to learn how to efficiently and effectively engage in the processes of learning. Although this need is not exclusive to individuals with LD or those who are at risk, addressing it in their curriculum does tend to be more critical for their growth as learners. One way students can increase the efficiency and effectiveness of their learning is to become more strategic. This text is specifically focused on how teachers and literacy providers can design instruction to teach learning strategies and the skills associated with them.

The position taken in this text is that strategy-based interventions designed for at-risk students should take place in strategic environments. The environment, which incorporates goals, expectations, resources, materials, and active learning, can affect the various dimensions of strategies instruction. Student success sought via strategy teaching can be achieved only when strategy curricula are taught through strategically rich instruction in environments that promote strategic learning.

This book focuses on how to effectively apply instruction in learning strategies to the teaching of adolescents with learning disabilities. Instruction in learning strategies, however, also is appropriate for adults with learning disabilities. Many instructors in adult literacy programs, postsecondary institutions, GED programs, and workplace training programs have found that the goals associated with learning strategy instruction also meet many of the needs of their students who learn differently. The variety and complexity of programs encountered across adult education settings, however, require a different level of innovation and flexibility in providing effective instruction than that demanded in most secondary school settings. Nevertheless, the basic instructional principles for promoting strategy acquisition and generalization described in this book are appropriate for teaching adults with learning disabilities. While the examples and references relate primarily to adolescents, adult educators are encouraged to study the instructional processes and principles and make appropriate modifications and translations to enhance instruction provided in adult education settings.

This book has been arranged in four parts. The first part presents a discussion of a number of issues and principles related to effective strategies instruction and describes strategies that will be used as examples throughout this text. The second part covers the instructional/learning stages of the Strategies Intervention Model (SIM) related to introducing and providing ongoing instruction in the acquisition of learning strategies. The third part addresses topics specifically related to strategy generalization and adaptation. The fourth part presents information on collaboration among support teachers and regular education content-area teachers for the infusion of learning strategies in content-area classes. Throughout the book many examples of statements teachers may make during specific instructional activities are provided. These are meant as examples only, to help the reader envision how the instruction might actually "look." You will be more competent at teaching using the SIM if you adapt it to your own language while keeping faithful to the practices that have made the SIM successful.

The SIM has its roots in the earlier days of special education under Public Law 94-142, The Education for All Handicapped Children Act. Special education has seen many innovations come and go since that historic law was passed. Significant among the changes is the nature of service to students with LD. At one time those who were fortunate got what assistance they could in a boiler room cum classroom. At another time these students received much of their education in pullout classrooms, virtually isolated from their "regular" peers throughout the entire school day. At times the typical special education curriculum for a student with LD was devoted to learning the basic skills of learning; content learning and the application of skills to authentic tasks were less common. Currently students with LD are increasingly being placed in mainstream content classrooms. In adult education settings, individuals with LD are rarely provided with separate instruction. However, they are expected to learn the same content as their peers. In many instances, unfortunately, inclusive education means that the amount of *special* education these students need in order to participate and benefit in the mainstream is neglected. In short, the nature of curricular demands and contexts for students with LD (indeed for all students) has changed significantly since the SIM was first developed.

This book presents the SIM as it has been validated, that is, as an instructional approach designed for students in support settings where they have time to focus on the process of strategic learning without a heavy concentration on content until the strategy is fairly well learned. We encourage the reader to recognize that in certain situations aspects of the SIM (e.g., devoting separate lessons to verbal rehearsal of strategy steps) may be difficult to accomplish. Innovations to make the model viable would be appropriate in such circumstances. We strongly caution, however, that when even a few changes are made in the SIM procedures, the effectiveness of the model may be jeopardized. Innovations do not need to be made purely in the SIM; for example, temporary schedule changes may sometimes be viable.

PART I

Critical Features of Effective Strategies Instruction

Features of Effective Strategies Instruction

O ver the past 15 years, direct teaching of strategies has progressed from the tight control of researchers working in laboratory settings (and artificially controlled classrooms) to the hands of teachers and students in classroom settings. Many teacher education programs now stress the importance of strategic learning. Publishers have begun to produce strategy-oriented teaching materials, and sessions on strategy-related interventions have become common at school in-services and professional conferences. Despite these efforts, however, the translation of strategy-related research into practice has often been poor. As a result, many of the strategy-oriented programs and materials currently in schools do not contribute to improved student strategicness or learning outcomes. Sadly, the story is much the same for teaching strategies to students with learning disabilities (LD). Research specifically on teaching strategies to students with LD has been ongoing since the mid- to late 1970s (e.g., Torgesen, 1977; Wong, 1979). The translation of this research into effective teaching practices has also been relatively limited. In many cases students with LD who learn strategies are as unlikely as their peers to use them independently and to generalize their use.

All is not bleak. Despite failures in strategy research and teaching, a number of successful strategy teaching[1] efforts have been empirically

---

[1]Pay careful attention to nomenclature. *Strategy teaching* refers to the teaching of strategies. As will be made clear in this text, there are a number of ways to teach strategies. *Strategic teaching* refers to types of teaching that are themselves strategic. One may teach strategically without teaching students a strategy, and vice versa.

developed and implemented by researchers and teacher trainers interested in improving the school performance and learning of students with LD and others performing poorly (e.g., Deshler & Schumaker, 1986; Lloyd & deBettencourt, 1982; Palincsar & Brown, 1984). In general, these efforts have included direct teaching or guided instruction, in which students are prompted to "establish goals, select appropriate procedures, and monitor progress towards achieving goals" (Mayer, 1987, p. 418). In these efforts, a strategy or set of strategies is identified that will enable a student to solve a specific problem (e.g., identifying a main idea). These strategy teaching efforts have generally required instruction over time (6 weeks to 1 year) with individuals and small groups (e.g., 3 to 6) of students. Many of these research-based strategy teaching efforts have led to enhanced performance and outcomes for students with LD.

Probably the most extensively researched and developed approach to direct strategy teaching for students with LD is the Strategies Intervention Model (SIM), developed by a group of researchers at the University of Kansas Institute for Research in Learning Disabilities (and since 1993, the Center for Research on Learning). Under the direction of Drs. Gordon Alley, Donald Deshler, and Jean Schumaker, a research and development staff has worked on various research projects primarily related to identification and intervention for adolescents and young adults with LD and their low-achieving peers. These research and development efforts have focused on identification and assessment issues, validation and replication of various components of the SIM, materials development and dissemination, teacher training, and the infusion of the model into education programs.

The purpose of this book is to identify the major components of effective strategy instruction that have emerged from research at the Institute for Research in Learning Disabilities and are reflected in the SIM, as well as from related research and development efforts by other researchers across a variety of fields.

THE CONCEPTS OF *STRATEGY* AND *STRATEGY INSTRUCTION*

The discussion of effective strategy instruction begins with defining *strategy* and *strategy instruction*. These are the basic concepts that have guided development of the SIM.

What a Strategy Is

The definition for a strategy that has been used in the development of the SIM is made clear in the following statement: *An individual's approach to a task is called a strategy when it includes how a person thinks and acts when planning, executing, and evaluating performance on a task and its outcomes.* The emphasis of this definition is on the approach used by a person to complete a task. The approach includes both cognitive (thinking process) and behavioral (overt actions) elements that guide student planning, performance, and evaluation of strategy engagement.

How a Strategy Differs from a Basic Academic Skill or Study Skill

Although it is possible to think of a strategy as a skill, in most school curricula a basic skill or a study skill consists of a set of steps or a procedure related to meeting a specific setting demand. This concept of a skill is often operationalized and taught through the specification of observable behaviors. For example, the steps that must be demonstrated in long division or to complete an outline can be listed and observed, and following them usually leads to a very specific outcome that documents completion of the task or some element of the task. These are not strategies; there is no accounting for how students plan, think about the observable and nonobservable behaviors, or evaluate their processes. A strategy consists of critical guidelines and rules related to selecting the best skills or procedures and making decisions about their use. Thus, while a strategy requires some type of skill knowledge, the focus is on the individual's approach to the task.

What Strategy Instruction Is

The goal of strategies instruction is to teach strategies in a manner that is effective (i.e., the strategy is learned and generalized by the student) and efficient (i.e., the strategy is learned to an optimal level with a minimum amount of effort by both the teacher and the student). Strategies instruction, then, is the teaching of strategies. This is different than strategic instruction, which is teaching in a strategic manner.

The Difference Between a Strategy and a Strategy Intervention

A strategy and a strategy intervention are quite different. The concept of *strategy* has emerged from cognitive psychology. Broadly speaking, cognitive psychologists have divided strategies into two domains: cognitive and metacognitive. Cognitive strategies relate to how an individual processes information. Metacognitive strategies relate to how an individual selects, monitors, and uses the cognitive strategies that he or she possesses. Whereas a strategy is a planful approach to a task, including both cognitive and metacognitive components, a strategy intervention is the application of a strategy or strategies to a meaningful task (e.g., a strategy to recall spelling rules applied when writing a book report).

Strategies do not become instructionally significant until they are associated with a specific task or problem (i.e., a strategy intervention). For example, a strategy for prioritizing becomes important only when it helps an individual solve a problem or complete a task in the context of meeting the demands or requirements presented by a specific setting. There are few academic tasks that require a single cognitive or metacognitive strategy. Important tasks, especially those that are important for the success of adolescents, often require a combination of cognitive and metacognitive strategies and substrategies. These combinations of strategies are referred to as *strategy systems*. As an example of a strategy system, the student writing the book report would likely apply not only a strategy for spelling but also strategies for organizing thoughts, writing coherent sentences, and checking the manuscript's overall quality. Most strategy intervention efforts do not consist of a single strategy but are actually strategy systems to meet the requirements of learning or performing across settings (e.g., a strategy designed to help a student develop mnemonic devices to help remember information may be combined with a method for accurately identifying and organizing the important information that needs to be remembered). When an intervention effort brings about a significant and practical magnitude of change (i.e., a change that parents, students, teachers, and administrators all recognize as positive and meaningful), it is difficult to selectively identify which aspects of the intervention contribute to the improvements, which aspects make no contribution, which aspects are inhibiting improvement, the interaction effect of various aspects, and what could have been added that would have contributed to an even greater magnitude of improvement.

The *spirit* of strategies instruction that must be created can be made apparent by examining the three dimensions that must be considered in order to provide effective strategies instruction. First, the teacher must have a clear concept of what constitutes an effective strategy intervention. This should include an understanding of (a) the nature or content of the strategy that is to be learned and (b) how the strategy content is organized or designed for learning by the student. Second, the teacher must know how to select a strategy for instruction. This should include an understanding of (a) the various types of strategies that match the demands that students must meet in order to be successful and (b) ways to determine the usefulness or transferability of the strategy for meeting demands and problems that the student must face. Third, the teacher must know how to teach strategies to students. To accomplish this the teacher must have knowledge of (a) the procedures that should be used to facilitate student acquisition and generalization of the strategy and (b) ways to create an instructional environment that will prompt and promote strategic learning and performance. Knowledge of these three dimensions is useful when a strategy intervention is being developed, when a strategy intervention is being compared with other types of interventions, and when a strategy is being considered for use with students.

How Strategy Acquisition Is Promoted

Current strategy teaching efforts range from direct to indirect teaching tactics. The direct teaching approach focuses on identifying an effective and efficient strategy for accomplishing a specific task and training the student in the strategy. Once the strategy is identified, the teacher instructs the student in the necessary skill prerequisites, presents the strategy, models the strategy, and provides direct practice opportunities and performance feedback to the student. On the other hand the indirect approach focuses on prompting student use of strategies through modeling, questioning, shaping, correcting, and interactively guiding student response to the task. In a direct approach the teacher guides the student through the task, gradually guiding the student to take responsibility for effective and efficient completion of the task. In some cases the teacher may never present a "best" strategy but rather helps the students to discover the best strategic approaches themselves. The primary difference between direct and indirect approaches, then, is in the role of the teacher. In the direct teaching approach, the strategy is made explicit and taught by the teacher. In the indirect approach the teacher leads the student toward knowledge and use of the strategy.

The teaching approach used in the SIM has changed over the years. Initially the focus of the instructional process was direct teaching of the strategy. Since the content of each strategy had been heavily researched and refined, the power of the strategy was thought to result in the intended outcomes. While it was found that students could be taught a given strategy or set of strategies, some students did not recognize the benefits of the strategy, were not highly motivated to learn the strategy, and were not generalizing strategies for academic success and personal use. As a result, through both formal and informal research, the instructional procedures specified for strategy instruction gradually changed to include an increased level of student involvement, participation, control, and commitment in the instructional process. These instructional procedures have been found to work best with individuals identified as being at risk for school failure, including those with LD. Thus the strategy teaching approach validated with the SIM may best be described as a direct strategy teaching approach incorporating indirect opportunities for the student to (a) become involved in the instructional process and (b) discover ways in which the strategy can be personally empowering. To maintain the integrity of the SIM teaching approach, specific teaching practices and instructional materials are made available only to teachers (and others) who participate in training workshops (see Appendix A). This decision has been made by the authors of SIM materials based on their research into what factors contribute to the fidelity of effective implementation.

EFFECTIVE STRATEGY INTERVENTIONS

Ellis and Lenz (1987) identified a number of critical features that should be considered when judging whether the spirit of strategies instruction is present in a direct strategy teaching intervention. These features relate to the content of the strategy and how the strategy is designed to enhance student learning.

Strategic Content

The content features of the strategy relate to how well the behavior and cognitive processes of meeting a task demand have been specified. The critical features that must be considered under this dimension concern the degree to which the strategy has incorporated principles of learning that have been found to facilitate a more effective and efficient response to meeting a demand. A strategy intervention may not contain all of these features; however, the intervention is more likely to be strategic when the following features are included in the intervention.

1. *The strategy should contain a set of steps that lead to a specific and successful outcome.* A strategy is not a collection of unorganized rules, characteristics, and guidelines that result in separate outcomes. A strategy consists of a set of steps that organizes the approach to a task and results in the successful completion of that task. Although individual units of performance may be evaluated, there is always one outcome that is used to judge the successfulness of the strategy (e.g., did the strategy help the student pass the test?). Using this outcome as a standard, the individual can examine the result of her or his effort and begin to evaluate the effectiveness of the strategy.

2. *The steps of the strategy should be sequenced in a manner that leads to an efficient approach to the task.* A strategy that simply leads to completion of a task is not enough. An efficient strategy is not merely a collection of good ideas organized into a set of steps. An efficient strategy is a collection of the "best" ideas organized into the "best" sequence that lead to the "best" cognitive and physical actions for the task. However, there is not always one single best approach. For example, what an adult thinks is the best approach to a task may not be best for the student. And what is best for one student may not be best for another. Whereas proficient readers often stop to check reading passage comprehension after chunks consisting of multiple paragraphs, readers struggling to improve comprehension often must stop at the end of much smaller chunks (e.g., at the end of each paragraph or even several times within a paragraph). Indeed, many expert readers find that stopping frequently to check comprehension often seems unnatural and inefficient. However, for immature readers, this if often the best approach.

3. *The steps of the strategy should cue the student to use specific cognitive strategies.* Most strategy interventions are actually strategy systems that include many cognitive strategies such as paraphrasing, clustering, and imaging. If the strategy does not include cues and explanations related to using cognitive strategies to approach tasks, it is likely that the strategy is simply a procedure with few strategic qualities.

4. *The steps of the strategy should cue the student to use metacognition.* The processes of reflection on the way that a task is being approached and evaluation of how it was accomplished are often difficult to identify in our own behavior. Therefore, we tend not to directly specify these metagcognitive processes when we develop interventions. Nonetheless, it is important to include these behaviors (e.g., self-questioning, self-evaluation, goal setting, checking, reviewing, self-monitoring) in the steps of the strategy when they are important to completing the task. These behaviors must be embedded in the steps of the strategy and explained to students if students are to be expected to use them.

5. *The steps of the strategy should cue the student to select and use appropriate procedures, skills, or rules.* A key function of a strategy is to guide the student to select the procedures, skills, and rules that are most appropriate for meeting the demands of a task. Therefore, the strategy must specifically inform the student as to which resources need to be applied and where. The strategy should name the appropriate procedure, skill, or rule and, if appropriate, include it as part of the strategy acquisition and generalization process. For example, if the student should use a specific division procedure to arrive at the correct answer to a problem, then this procedure should be specified along with specific instructions about how to think and make decisions about the procedure.

6. *The steps of the strategy should cue the student to perform some type of overt physical action.* A strategy must cue both cognitive actions (e.g., evaluate importance of information) and physical actions (e.g., list important information). An absence of physical actions from the strategy steps will make it difficult for the individual and the teacher to evaluate application of the strategy and monitor progress toward meeting the setting demand.

7. *All of the overt physical actions should be supported by a clear explanation of the associated cognitive actions that need to take place.* Every critical physical action should be associated with cognitive actions. Explanations or information about cognitive actions provide guidance related to decisions about the best way to meet the demand. For example, if the steps of the strategy cue the student to take notes, then the explanation for that cue should provide guidance in how to make decisions about what information should be written as notes.

8. *All of the steps of the strategy should be able to be performed by an individual in a limited amount of time.* The steps of the strategy need to be balanced in relation to when they are to be performed. Usually a strategy must be performed in a reasonably short period of time. Strategies that must be performed over an extended period of time often undermine the self-instruction process (are forgotten) and can be ineffective. Frequently strategies that cover tasks that extend over a long period of time, such as 1 or 2 days, suffer from insufficient analysis of the task or demand. Strategies that attempt to address such tasks, such as homework completion, must take into consideration that there are probably many strategies involved, not only one.

9. *Unnecessary steps or explanations should be eliminated.* The number of steps and the amount of explanation in the strategy need to be no more than what is needed to enable the individual to learn the strategy and meet the setting demands. Therefore, the content must be reviewed, and information that might be trivial to the task or unnecessarily increase the amount of information that must be remembered may need to be omitted. Cues to sharpen the pencil or turn the page are examples of steps that may be unnecessary.

10. *Information related to why to use the strategy, when to use the strategy, and where to use the strategy should be included.* The knowledge of the situational conditions under which the strategy should be used is as much a part of the strategy as is knowledge of the specific steps. Rationales that include information related to specific, personal, believable, and short-term consequences for use and nonuse of the strategy should be taught. In addition, identifying the characteristics of situations where the strategy should also be used and the cues that will help the student identify these situations will help to promote appropriate use and subsequent generalization of the strategy.

11. *The strategy should provide guidelines related to how to think and act when planning, executing, and evaluating performance on a task and its outcomes.* Through the features described above, the complete strategy should promote the processes of planning, executing, and evaluating. The strategy should guide the individual's approach to the task while promoting strategy flexibility that will enable the student to meet unexpected circumstances and situations related to a task. The teacher should review the entire strategy and evaluate whether attention to the content features described above has accomplished this. If not, then the strategy should be modified to meet these conditions.

Strategic Design

The strategy should be designed or packaged in a manner that successfully organizes and arranges its content for optimal learning and use by the student. The critical features of strategic design concern how understanding and memory of the strategy are facilitated through the presentation and arrangement of the strategy content. A strategy intervention is more likely to be learned and generalized if the following design features are included in the intervention.

1. *Entry-level skills should be clearly specified or taken into consideration as part of the steps of the strategy.* A strategy often informs an individual as to how to apply skills. Therefore, the skill abilities or skill proficiency levels that are prerequisite to strategy performance must be clearly specified. Any skills that are not specified as a prerequisite should be "learnable" within the intervention process. The teacher must decide either to teach any entry-level skills that are required so a particular strategy can be taught or to implement another intervention. For example, if the strategy requires independent use of a dictionary or a glossary, the student should be taught how to use a dictionary or glossary before instruction in the strategy begins; if not, this instruction should be a part of strategy instruction.

2. *A remembering system should be incorporated into the intervention to facilitate memorization of strategy steps.* Because the content of a strategy (e.g., cues, rationales, procedures) can be elaborate, and many individuals who require direct strategy teaching need assistance in learning and remembering information, the design of the strategy must facilitate the process of memorizing content. There should be a set of key action words that an individual learns and memorizes that will trigger the appropriate associations or explanations related to successful performance of a strategy. For example, "Decide on audience, goals, and position" cues a student to identify a perspective before beginning to write when using the DEFENDS Writing Strategy (Ellis, 1994). Also, the content of the strat-

egy should be organized for easy remembering, and a mnemonic device should be developed as part of the strategy intervention. The mnemonic device used in DEFENDS, for example, cues students as to the steps of the strategy and reminds them to talk to themselves as part of performing each step. This design feature can reduce the memorization load and allow the student to focus on understanding and applying the strategy.

3. *Each step of the remembering system should be short.* As each step of the remembering system is formed, unnecessary words should be eliminated. This is to keep the load of information to be memorized at a minimum. Every attempt should be made to select a few key action words that will facilitate a direct association to the critical cognitive and physical actions that are necessary for completion of a step. "Decide on audience, goals, and position" demonstrates this feature.

4. *Each step of the remembering system should begin with a verb or a key word directly related to the cognitive or physical action that the step cues.* Beginning each strategy step with a verb helps promote an active approach to the task. Steps are often more easily remembered when each step begins with an action word. Steps that begin with words such as *the, if, then,* and *which* do not have the power of steps starting with words such as *write, find, look, ask,* and *choose.* It is also helpful if all the steps use a parallel language structure. For example, if one of the steps begins with a verb and is written in the first person singular, all steps should follow that style.

5. *There should be seven or fewer key steps in the remembering system for the strategy.* The memory load of a strategy increases as the number of steps in the strategy increases. Research on memory has been helpful in determining that most individuals remember on average 7 (plus or minus 2) units of information. The complexity of the information and how logically it is perceived as relating can influence just how much is remembered. Therefore, for ease of strategy recall, the number of steps should be limited to seven or less. Some tasks, however, require a much more sophisticated strategy and, as a result, more steps. If this occurs, ways of embedding a substrategy or a ministrategy within a general set of steps might be helpful. For example, there may be five steps to a strategy, but in the fourth step there may be a cue to perform a short three-step substrategy before going on to the fifth general step of the strategy. Using this tactic more efficiently organizes the strategy and makes it easier to remember and perform. For example, in the DEFENDS strategy (Ellis, 1994) the "S" step is further broken down into the substrategy SEARCH.

6. *The remembering system should relate to the overall process that the strategy is designed to address.* When a mnemonic device is used to promote remembering the strategy, it is helpful if the mnemonic word or image is closely related to the strategic process desired. For example, a strategy related to homework with the mnemonic device ASSIGN (Rademacher, 1993) may be more easily remembered and trigger the appropriate strategy than the mnemonic device BOAT. The mnemonic device BOAT could cue the student to recall that the strategy will lead to "smooth sailing" through homework assignments, but BOAT is probably less easily associated with homework than ASSIGN and should therefore be avoided. Although many strategies have been developed and are successful without relying on a mnemonic device related to the process, this feature can make the strategy easier to learn and remember for some students.

7. *The language and vocabulary used to convey the strategy steps and explanations should be uncomplicated and familiar.* As in any intervention, the words selected to teach the strategy should be carefully selected. The words generally should be familiar and easy to understand. However, it is critical that the remembering system consist of words that are powerful and meaningful to the student. When essential words are unfamiliar to a student, learning them should be included as part of the teaching process.

SELECTING STRATEGIES FOR INSTRUCTION
Knowledge, Motivation, and Strategy Instruction

Successful strategy instruction can be characterized as both intensive and extensive (Pressley, Goodchild, Fleet, Zajchowski, & Evans, 1989). That is, strategy instruction focuses on promoting the effective and efficient integration of various types of information or knowledge required to complete a task. Ellis, Deshler, Lenz, Schumaker, and Clark (1991) argued that successful learning and performance in a classroom setting is contingent on the type and level of knowledge possessed by a student across four critical domains. These domains are (a) process knowledge, (b) procedural knowledge, (c) conditional knowledge, and (d) semantic knowledge. Process knowledge is awareness of the essential cognitive and metacognitive strategies required for problem solving. Procedural knowledge is understanding how skills and strategies are organized to promote successful task completion. Process and procedural knowledge are the two areas that are usually thought of as constituting the knowledge of the steps and actions related to implementing a strategy. Conditional knowledge is related to judging when and how strategies should be applied. This type of knowledge is strongly related to a student's ability to generalize a strategy and, unfortunately, it is an area that is often neglected in strategy instruction. Attention to and instruction in this aspect of the strategy may often be neglected because it requires exploration, reflection, and discussion of the application of the strategy over time. Semantic knowledge is related to what the student already knows and can automatically access for use in problem solving. It includes both the prerequisite knowledge of skills that must be used to perform a strategy and the information about a topic that must be utilized in the problem-solving process. For example, for a student who is paraphrasing to aid comprehension of a passage on photosynthesis, semantic knowledge would include the decoding skills needed to read the words and what the student already knows about the sun and plant life, which are used to help make the passage meaningful.

Consideration of the four knowledge domains is critical when selecting strategies for instruction. The teacher not only must decide what types of strategies are needed to help the student meet specific setting demands, but also must determine the conditions under which the strategy must be applied and the types of knowledge and skills the student must already possess to learn and use the strategy.

Strategy Usefulness

Although many strategies could be taught to a student, no student needs to learn all of the strategies that one might have to teach. The selection of a strategy based on its relevance to the needs of the student is an important part of the strategy intervention process. Three conditions are potentially important to determining the appropriateness of a strategy intervention. The critical features that must be considered across these conditions relate to the potential use and transferability of the strategy across materials, people, settings, situations, and time. Although a strategy may not meet all of these conditions, an intervention is likely to be successful if the following conditions are met:

1. *The strategy should address a key problem that is found in settings that the student must face.* When strategies are immediately useful and the benefits of their use are readily apparent, they tend to be learned and generalized more quickly than those that are useful only in future circumstances or those for which the student perceives little value. For example, although reading is an important overall skill, if the students are not expected to read for information in content-area classes (e.g., the content instead is presented primarily through class discussions), the students are less likely to be motivated to learn reading strategies. Likewise, students should be able to recognize a relationship between the effort applied to learn a strategy and their success when using it.

2. *The strategy should relate to frequently required demands, ideally those that occur across settings.* The more opportunities that a student has to apply the strategy, the more likely the student will be to learn the strategy quickly, see the benefits of the strategy, attribute success in meeting specific demands to application of the strategy, and habitualize its use. Therefore, when selecting which strategies to teach, a key consideration is the degree to which the student will have an opportunity to apply each strategy and integrate it into his or her overall approach to solving problems. Whenever possible each strategy's use should be prompted in a variety of settings, situations, and contexts.

3. *The strategy must be generalizable across a variety of settings, situations, and contexts.* Although a strategy can be developed for a very specific situation, those strategies that have the greatest generalization potential can be used across situations and settings. For example, the Paraphrasing Strategy (Schumaker, Denton, & Deshler, 1984), a reading comprehension strategy, can be applied in almost every setting and content area that requires reading. Therefore, this strategy is highly generalizable. However, suppose the Paraphrasing Strategy were altered to make the steps relate only to reading and paraphrasing science content. Although the strategy would then be very effective for reading science material, the student's application of the strategy to other content areas would become difficult.

Strategic Instruction

Once the content, design, and usefulness of a strategy have been determined, the strategy must be taught to the student. Strategic instruction promotes the active participation of the student in the learning process. The goal is to immerse the student in an instructional situation in which learning is seen as a vehicle to realize personal goals. The student is involved in making decisions about what is to be learned and how quickly learning will occur. Specific stages for promoting successful strategy acquisition and generalization have been developed by researchers at the University of Kansas Institute for Research in Learning Disabilities (Alley & Deshler, 1979; Ellis et al., 1991). The eight stages of this instructional process are presented in Figure 1.1.

These stages of strategy instruction are designed to achieve a balance between the teacher's control and the student's control of the learning process. Other strategy training efforts may emphasize one type of control over another. However, even though strategy learning may be achieved through instruction that is more teacher directed or through instruction that is more student directed, the following general instructional features appear to be central to successful strategy instruction:

1. *The student should commit to learn the strategy and fully understand the purpose and benefits of the strategy.* The student's understanding of the potential impact of the strategy and the consequences of continued use of ineffective and inefficient strategies should be the first step in the instructional process. The student should be committed to learn the strategy and understand how the strategy can have an immediate impact on success. Therefore, the teacher must be responsible for helping the student to recognize the goals of the strategy and for obtaining a commitment from the student to learn the strategy. This is a frequently overlooked aspect of teaching. Likewise, the teacher must demonstrate to the student that she or he is committed to helping the student to acquire and generalize the strategy.

2. *The physical and cognitive actions covered in the strategy should be fully described and explained.* The student should be informed as to what to do and how to think about each step of the strategy. Otherwise the strategy will be a meaningless routine of steps the student follows with little thought. The full content of the strategy should be made apparent to the student. Examples and circumstances relevant to the student's experiences should be incorporated into the presentation, and the student should play an active role in exploring and commenting on the strategy and its uses. In addition, the teacher should ensure that students understand when and where to use the strategy and how to identify cues that signal appropriate and timely use.

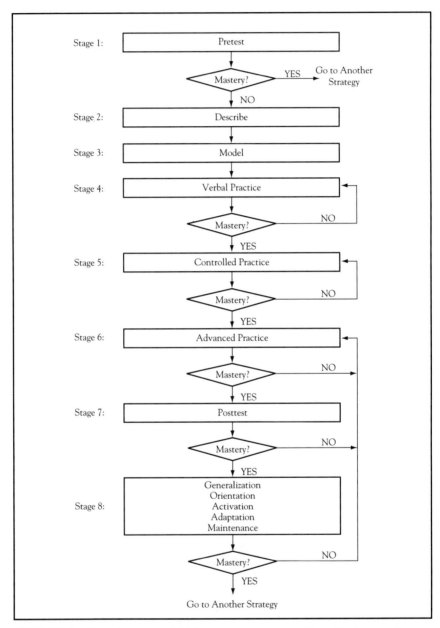

FIGURE 1.1. The eight stages of SIM strategies instruction. From *The Learning Strategies Curriculum: The Paraphrasing Strategy* (p. 4), by J. B. Schumaker, P. H. Denton, and D. D. Deshler, 1984, Lawrence: University of Kansas, Institute for Research in Learning Disabilities. Copyright 1984 by Schumaker, Denton, and Deshler. Reprinted with permission.

3. *To facilitate the process of self-instruction, the student should be informed as to how to use the remembering system incorporated in the strategy intervention.* Once the content of the strategy has been presented to the student, the teacher should demonstrate how the strategy can be easily remembered using its remembering system. In the SIM, each step of the strategy is easily remembered using a mnemonic cue word (e.g., FIRST). The teacher should explicitly relate the steps of the remembering system to the intended physical and cognitive associations and teach the student how to use the remembering system in the self-instruction process. This step addresses the memory difficulties exhibited by many low-achieving students.

4. *The student should understand the process of learning the strategy and should participate in goal-setting activities in order to anticipate and monitor learning.* The student should (a) be informed of the acquisition and generalization process, (b) understand the goals and vocabulary associated with each strategy step, and (c) set goals for mastery of each step. As instruction proceeds, the student should evaluate completion of each step to determine if specified learning goals have been met. If not, the student should initiate feedback to the teacher on which aspects of learning goals have not been met. During the instructional process, the student should become an active facilitator and evaluator of the successfulness of the instruction. In addition, the student must be taught to become a collaborator in identifying and addressing failures in strategy learning.

5. *Multiple models of the strategy should be provided; an appropriate balance between the physical and cognitive activities involved in the strategy should be achieved.* The heart of strategic instruction is the "think-aloud" model presented by the teacher. This model must present an accurate and complete demonstration of the application of the strategy. Although a complete and thorough initial model is critical, additional modeling episodes should occur throughout the instructional process. In each of these models, the physical activities must be demonstrated as the associated cognitive activities are made apparent in an overt think-aloud depiction of the strategy.

6. *The student should be enlisted in the model and become a full participant in guiding the strategy instructional process.* From the beginning the student should be invited to participate in the modeling. For example, upon identifying the clues to the main idea of a reading, the teacher may ask the student to then model naming the main idea.

7. *The strategy should be fully understood and memorized before practice is initiated.* Sufficient rehearsal of the strategy steps should be provided before the student is asked to perform the strategy from memory. Before applied practice of the strategy begins, students should know the remembering system, be able to demonstrate how they can use the remembering system to guide the self-instruction process in applying the strategy, paraphrase or explain what is involved in each step, provide personal rationales for learning and using the strategy, and accurately answer questions about uses and misuses of the strategy across various conditions. During the forthcoming practice phase, students must be confident in their knowledge of the strategy and be able to concentrate on the application of the strategy without having to focus unnecessary cognitive effort on remembering the strategy steps.

8. *Practice should begin with controlled guided practice and ultimately conclude with advanced independent practice.* The goal of the initial practice stage should be mastering the strategy without having to struggle with content or situational demands. Therefore, practice should be provided under conditions in which the student is comfortable or knowledgeable. The content used, however, should be that with which the strategy will eventually be applied. As the strategy is learned, conditions that approximate actual setting and task demands should be gradually introduced. While general principles of effective teaching should be used, the most important teaching behaviors during strategy practice appear to include communicating expectations, ensuring intensity of instruction, requiring mastery, and providing feedback.

9. *A measurement system should be used as a source of ongoing information that will demonstrate to the student and the teacher that the strategy is being learned and used and that the demands of the setting are being met.* Knowledge of progress and performance is a critical part of the learning process. The measurement system should provide information to the student on whether the strategy is helping in terms of promoting success in meeting a demand. However, the measurement system should also provide information related to the student's mastery of the strategy. Progress in learning the strategy should eventually relate to an increase in the student's ability to meet a setting demand or some aspect of a setting demand. Students should be able to see this relationship and attribute success to mastery and application of the strategy. A simple way to achieve this is to have students graph their own strategy performance and resultant learning when possible and then reflect on what the graph shows.

10. *Specific efforts to promote generalization should follow strategy acquisition.* After the strategy has been mastered, the student should once again make a commitment. While generalization should be promoted throughout the strategy acquisition process, this second commitment should be focused on generalizing the strategy. In the generalization stage, the teacher and student work together to identify where the strategy can be used across settings and conditions, identify modifications in the strategy to make it more generalizable, and plan for use of the strategy across settings. The generalization process can be greatly enhanced through the cooperation of as many teachers and other facilitators as possible.

Creating a Strategic Environment

The critical features of direct strategy teaching that have been described thus far represent a very specific method for promoting strategy acquisition and generalization that has been demonstrated to be effective for many students with LD and for many students at risk for school failure (Schumaker & Deshler, 1992). If one were to examine only the separate learning strategies, the features of SIM could be viewed as representing a rather limited perspective on strategies teaching. One could reasonably argue that under SIM the spirit of strategies instruction has been considered only at the single intervention level. The key to delivering a truly strategic intervention using SIM, however, is to not conceptualize strategies instruction as consisting of a single or several strategy interventions, or even as a well-developed strategies curriculum. In SIM, strategies interventions consist of the creation of an environment in which everything that is done is done in a strategic manner. A strategic environment is created when all individuals involved in the education process, including teachers, students, and parents or guardians, promote, model, guide, and prompt strategic learning and performance across all settings. The following list of characteristics represents current thinking on the type of instructional environment that can potentially maximize strategic learning and performance.

1. *Participants believe in the value of creating a strategic environment.* What individuals believe about the setting in which learning takes place may be as important as or more important than the instruction itself (Lenz & Deshler, 1990). Beliefs include the perceptions and expectations of a situation that an individual holds. To create and maintain a strategic

environment, the teacher must believe that the goal of instruction includes the attainment of knowledge and that a large part of that body of knowledge includes how to think and how to be both independent and interdependent when solving problems. The teacher should teach in a manner consistent with these beliefs and arrange situations in which these beliefs can be reflected in both the teacher's and students' procedures. The effective strategies teacher, therefore, must take advantage of instructional situations outside of direct strategy instruction to prompt independent, cooperative, and collaborative strategic performance. This atmosphere can be communicated in the manner in which students complete assignments and the ways in which discussion and feedback sessions are held. Teachers who are successful in creating a strategic environment tend to use instructional materials and manuals as a means to an end rather than as an end in themselves (Deshler & Lenz, 1989). That is, the instructional goal is development of strategicness and not merely completion of a task.

2. *Learning is driven by student goals and plans.* Students must be able to recognize the relationships among learning a specific type of knowledge, applying this knowledge, and the successes resulting from correct use of this knowledge. However, the resulting performance must be within the student's value system. If it is not, the student will not be likely to want to continue to participate in learning; as a result, motivation will decrease. In summary, a teacher is successful in creating a strategic environment when students understand how learning takes place, have knowledge of the instructional process, and have opportunities to select and make decisions about what they learn. This process can be abetted by student participation in both selection of goals and planning to attain those goals.

3. *Strategy instruction revolves around the demands of mainstream classes.* Historically, the goal of instruction in remedial and support classes has revolved around increasing students' performance of academic skills. For example, if the student has difficulty in reading comprehension, the goal of instruction would be to increase reading skills such as using context clues; if the student does not know how to outline, the goal of instruction is to teach the student how to outline. However, as students with LD progress to higher grade levels and are included in the mainstream classroom, the criteria for success becomes more focused on success with content-area class assignments (Scanlon, Schumaker, & Deshler, 1994). The changing academic demands on students with LD preclude

instruction devoted largely to the processes of learning. Successful learning in such an environment requires student independence (Jones, Palincsar, Ogle, & Carr, 1987). Students' personal satisfaction often increases when success is earned independently, that is, without the assistance of tutoring or curricular modifications. A strategic environment, then, is focused on activities and decisions related to teaching students how to independently and strategically meet the current demands of the mainstream setting.

4. *Students are expected to chart and monitor their own progress.* Students must learn to make decisions daily based on knowledge of what they have accomplished, what mistakes they are making, and how much time they have left to accomplish goals. This process helps students learn to manage time, make decisions promptly, and maintain a goal-oriented perspective. A visual depiction of performance assists students in evaluating their performance. In addition to their being taught and prompted to be involved in the progress management aspects of learning, students should be taught the criteria for evaluation and how to determine when they need to seek assistance from peers or their teacher.

5. *Support teachers spend the majority of their time modeling strategic learning and providing elaborated feedback.* Although it may seem logical that the majority of time spent in a strategic environment would be spent in the direct instruction of strategies, this is not the case. Strategies would be much easier to teach if this were the case. Indeed, only a small portion of the time is spent in the direct explanation of strategies. The majority of time must be spent in helping students understand the strategies and apply them in useful contexts. This process is done primarily through the frequent and automatic use of good modeling and elaborated feedback. Indeed, the teacher should be modeling strategic performance as part of both group and individual feedback sessions.

6. *The learning process is viewed as being interactive and reciprocal.* There is always the question of how much of the instructional process should be teacher directed and how much should be student directed. A strategic environment is created when the teacher directs the learning process as an expert guide, leading students to the edge of what they already know and then prompting them to begin building a bridge (or bridges) to other knowledge and contexts. This building process may best be facilitated through an interactive process in which students and teachers explore relationships, make hypotheses, test hypotheses, draw conclusions, and apply information. The teacher plays a major role in presenting important knowledge required of students and in guiding the learning process. Through this process teachers learn how students think about learning. They therefore can more readily guide students into the next logical phase of instruction. Instructional steps and procedures serve as a framework for ordering and organizing instruction in an effective and efficient manner. The quality of the instructional interaction within each stage of the instructional process, however, rests largely in the degree to which a teacher uses the knowledge of students, the curriculum, and the instructional environment to extend instruction in an interactive and reciprocal manner.

7. *All participants prompt strategic learning.* In the process of creating a strategic environment, all participants—special education teacher, student, mainstream teacher, and parent or guardian—must play active roles in promoting strategic learning. The more strategy learning becomes valued by all participants in the learning process, the more likely it is that specific actions to promote strategic learning will be taken. Participants' roles may simply be prompting the use of either specific or general strategies. For the mainstream teacher, strategic learning may be prompted by presenting content in a manner that can be better understood and remembered by students. The mainstream teacher should encourage a strategic approach to the content. Students may prompt, cue, or teach other students. Parents and guardians may be involved in prompting generalization of strategies.

8. *Instruction is specific, explicit, intensive, extensive, personalized, individualized, and action oriented.* Although the infusion of any strategy instruction across educational settings would go a long way to improve strategic performance, direct instruction in strategies is required to have an impact on performance. Strategies taught over a long period of time appear to have the greatest impact on student performance, indicating that an environment should be created that allows for extensive instruction in strategies. The environment must allow for instruction that is personalized and individualized so that individual goals and problems can be addressed and feedback can be provided. Finally, the instructional environment must be organized to allow students to explore strategies across a variety of contexts so that they can see that strategy learning is action oriented and can be used to address problems across situations and settings.

In summary, while an awful lot seems to be involved in efficient and effective strategy teaching, it is not unlike riding a bicycle, in that each step in the process makes a critical contribution to the process but is of limited use without performance of the others. And also, just like riding a bicycle, attending to all of the important features of strategy teaching becomes fairly automatic with practice and in no time seems to be one fluid process. Efficient and effective strategy teaching is teaching that accounts for all features that contribute to students efficiently and effectively *learning* strategies. Strategies that students learn should be responses to complex demands, which is why they are most effective when applied as part of a strategy system. A strategy to prioritize content of a story, for example, is of little use to a student when it is learned in isolation; rarely does a person have reason just to prioritize the content of a story. Even in school, that skill is learned and practiced in larger contexts, such as composing and producing stories or comprehending a story. Thus, to satisfy the spirit of efficient and effective strategy teaching, both the strategies that are learned and the methods used to teach them need to take into account the multiplicity of features that critically influence how they are learned and applied.

Example Strategies

2

Strategies exist for virtually all academic-related areas in which a person could have some skills. Some strategies are related to learning, others to motivation, and still others to areas such as social skills. Within the SIM learning strategies, there are three specific types, or strands, of learning strategies: *acquisition strategies* are used for the assimilation and accommodation of information; *storage strategies* are used to transform and manipulate information once it has been assimilated and accommodated; and *demonstration and expression of knowledge strategies* are used to communicate one's knowledge. Learning strategies from each of the three strands can help students to meet the academic demands of school. Not all students need to learn specific strategies from all three strands; nor is competency at a strategy from any one strand necessarily prerequisite to competency at one from another strand.

To present all of the SIM learning strategies that might be beneficial for students is beyond the scope of this text. Three strategies have been selected as representative examples; they will be referred to throughout the book. The first two, Paraphrasing and FIRST-Letter Mnemonic, are published as parts of the SIM series; the third, DEFENDS, which is not part of the SIM series, is not yet published but follows SIM guidelines. (Appendix A provides a list of sources related to identifying additional strategies and strategy-related materials.) The three strategies are presented in this book in excerpted form—the first two in overview form, the third in more detail—from instructional manuals that contain comprehensive and detailed information regarding how to teach them to students and how to evaluate student performance. Details of the strategies, procedures, and materials are available only to individuals who participate in training workshops. In all cases, the procedures presented here reflect only the general guidelines for how these strategies are best taught. The procedures are presented in the form of scripts so that you may read examples of how a teacher would present them to students. Although scripts are useful as models of how to present a strategy, effective teachers need to present strategies in the same format but using their own language and not follow the wording of the scripts.

PARAPHRASING: A STRATEGY FOR IMPROVING READING COMPREHENSION

The Paraphrasing Strategy (Schumaker, Denton, & Deshler, 1984) has been taught to students to help them improve their reading comprehension by paraphrasing what they read. It is from the acquisition strand of SIM strategies. Paraphrasing is the process of restating the meaning of a passage in words other than those originally used. Through paraphrasing students are challenged to reflect upon what they comprehend. As was discussed in Chapter 1, most effective strategy interventions do not consist of only one cognitive strategy but are actually strategy systems that comprise a number of procedures and processes. This is certainly true of the Paraphrasing Strategy.

Teaching the Paraphrasing Strategy

To introduce the Paraphrasing Strategy to students, a teacher might say something such as the following:

> When you read a school assignment, a newspaper article, or instructions for something at home or work, you need to understand and remember what you read. To help yourself understand and remember, you should stop as you are reading and check to make sure that you are understanding.

You are going to learn a strategy that will help you understand and remember more of what you read. It gives you a way to stop and think about what you are reading while you are reading it. The strategy is called the Paraphrasing Strategy. To paraphrase means to put information into your own words. A good way to be sure you are understanding what you are reading is to put it in your own words. If you can't put it in your own words, you haven't understood it well. When you have something to read, the first thing you are going to do is carefully read the first paragraph. As you read you should think about what you are reading. At the end of the paragraph, stop reading. You want to stop and check to make sure you have understood and can remember what you've read so far. If you go on to the next paragraph before you understand the first one, chances are pretty good that you won't be able to understand what you read next.

When you stop reading, ask yourself what this paragraph is about. You will learn some specific questions to ask yourself that will help you to make that decision. These questions will help you to find main ideas and important details. The main idea presents the "big picture" or is a statement that summarizes the most important information in the paragraph. Each paragraph has its own main idea. The only exceptions to this are extremely short paragraphs. You will also learn to ask yourself questions that help you to identify important details to remember.

After you have decided on the main idea and details, you should state, in your own words, what they are. This is the third step, the actual paraphrasing. Later you will be asking the questions and saying the paraphrases to yourself, but for now I want you to practice describing the main idea and details to me, to the other students in the class, and on a tape recorder. Let's talk about how you state what you think the main idea and details are in your own words. You have to think of different words to say the same thing. The way you word it should be clear. For example, look at this sample paragraph [distribute copies or place on an overhead]:

Original Information

On May 31, 1889, the collapse of the Conemaugh Reservoir resulted in the great Jamestown Flood. The collapse of the dam resulted in the disastrous flooding of the Pennsylvania town of Jamestown, which was located southeast of Pittsburgh.

More than 2,000 people were killed, and damage was estimated at $10,000,000. It was charged that the dam holding back the waters was badly constructed. However, the state legislature of Pennsylvania never investigated.

Paraphrased Information

"The main thing this paragraph tells me is that the collapse of a poorly built dam may have caused the flood that killed thousands of people in Jamestown, Pennsylvania, in 1889. Some of the important details are that in the flood, 2,000 people died, the cost of the damage was over $10,000,000, and government officials did nothing to find out why the dam did not hold."

After you have paraphrased the information to yourself, to someone else, or into the tape recorder, you should continue by beginning to read the next paragraph. As you start the next paragraph you should again cue yourself to use your Paraphrasing Strategy following the steps we will learn.

A remembering system has been designed to assist the student in remembering the Paraphrasing Strategy steps. A mnemonic device in the form of an acronym is used. Each letter of the acronym stands for a step of the strategy. Once students have been introduced to the remembering system, they are taught how to associate the remembering system to the strategy and to the outcomes that are to be achieved by using the strategy.

FIRST-LETTER MNEMONIC: A STRATEGY FOR MEMORIZING LISTS

The FIRST-Letter Mnemonic Strategy (Nagel, Schumaker, & Deshler, 1986) has been useful in helping students memorize information for purposes such as tests. It is an example of a storage strand strategy. Using the FIRST-Letter Mnemonic Strategy, students improve how they (a) find lists of important information in texts and notes and (b) organize that information into memorable lists, as well as (c) develop a personalized remembering system and (d) engage in a self-study process to memorize the information. There are two phases to the implementation of this strategy. First students are taught how to create mnemonic devices for remembering information. After they have learned this process, they are taught how to review texts and notes for the purpose of fitting the use of mnemonics into the process of studying and self-testing. This strategy is very sophisticated; it requires the student to be able to read and understand information in text or notes in order to create lists to be remembered. Only the part of the strategy that focuses on teaching students how to create a mnemonic device for lists that have already been created will be overviewed here.

Teaching the FIRST-Letter Mnemonic Strategy

To teach the FIRST-Letter Mnemonic Strategy to students, the teacher might say something such as the following:

Often, just understanding information as you read or hear it is not enough. You also have to remember that information. In school we often expect you to demonstrate on a test that you remember information. Information can be best remembered when it is organized. Forming lists is one way that we can organize information. By making lists we can put the information into meaningful groups. Once we organize information into such lists we can study and memorize it more easily.

Organized lists have two major parts. First, a list has a heading that states what its main idea is, or what all the items have in common. Second, a list contains several items related to that heading. The items in a list can be thought of as details that support or explain the main idea. If you have a list of items to remember that have nothing in common, there is a problem. Either you don't understand yet what they have in common, or there is no reason you should be remembering those items at the same time. (Of course, that is different than having more than one list to remember at the same time.) We are going to learn a strategy that will help you to organize and memorize lists.

Being able to memorize lists can be very helpful. If you are able to remember a list of the important parts of something, you can use that list whenever you need to know the information—for example, to answer a test question. Because many tasks require you to follow a set of procedures or to complete the task in a certain way, a memorized list of the procedure steps can help you complete the task efficiently and accurately.

One of the best ways to remember things is to use a mnemonic device. A mnemonic device is a learning trick or tool that is used to help you remember. You are going to learn a strategy that will help you to create and use your own mnemonic devices. The mnemonic device that you are going to learn uses the first letter of each item in a list to help you remember the whole list. This strategy is called the FIRST-Letter Mnemonic Strategy; we will learn to call it the FIRST Strategy. I will explain more about that later.

After you have learned how to use the FIRST-Letter mnemonic technique, I will teach you how to identify and construct good lists as you study. To start, though, we want to focus on how to memorize lists that we already have.

In order to create a first-letter mnemonic, you must have a list. I have a list here that I found in a science book:

Glands in the Exocrine System

pancreas	ovaries
pituitary	testes
hypothalamus	thyroid
adrenal	

In trying to develop a mnemonic device for this list, the first thing that you should do is look to see if the first letters of each of the items form a word. The first letters of the items printed horizontally look like this:

P P H A O T T

If the first letters of each item forms a word, then the word can be used as a mnemonic device when you study. In our list, however, the first letters of each item do not form a word. If this first step does not work, then you need to look at the first letters of each item and see if the letters are close to forming a word. Maybe you can form a word by inserting one or two letters. When you insert a letter to form a word, insert it as a lowercase letter so that you don't confuse the inserted letter with one of the letters that stand for one of the items in your list. For example, in the provided list, we could insert a lowercase e *between the two Ps and an o between the two Ts to form the words PeP and ToT. But this does not help us remember the rest of the items. So this step does not work on this list very well.*

If this does not work, you can try to rearrange the items in the list. You can only do this if sequence is not essential to your list (e.g., a procedure that must be done in a certain order). To do this, simply try rearranging the letters in various orders until you can form a word. We can do this with the list that has been provided:

P P H A O T T can become T O P P H A T

The word TOPP has an extra p, but that is not a problem. Once you have a mnemonic, you can go on to another list you must memorize and create a mnemonic for it. Sometimes, however, you cannot form a word out of the first letters of each of the listed items using the three steps described above. If the efforts described above fail, you can try to create an interesting sentence using the first letter of the list items as the first letter for each word in the sentence. This step is especially helpful when the items cannot be rearranged. Let's pretend that the letters P P H A O T T cannot be arranged. The sentence that you might create could look something like this:

Party Poopers Hate Allowing Others To Tickle.

If all of these procedures fail, you can try various combinations of the procedures. For example, rearrange the letters and add one or two lowercase letters. You may need to brainstorm and use your imagination here. Maybe you can use a mnemonic word within a sentence or rearrange the letters to form a sentence that might be more personally meaningful or memorable. For example, you can use the names of friends in your sentence:

Tell Tina Only About How Peter Plays.

In summary, whenever you are presented with a list that is important for you to remember, this should be the cue to use the FIRST Strategy. These lists can be made for information to remember at school, at home, and at work.

Just as with the Paraphrasing Strategy, a remembering system has been designed to facilitate student organization in using the strategy and to help students to remember the steps of the process. The student must, however, understand the process described above before the remembering system becomes useful. The remembering system is itself a mnemonic device in which each letter of the word FIRST signals a step of the strategy.

Once students have been introduced to the remembering system, they need to be taught how to associate the remembering system with the strategy and to the outcomes that are to be achieved by using the strategy. An example of the association between the remembering system and the content of the FIRST-Letter Mnemonic Strategy you might share with your students is:

> *The word FIRST should help you remember how to use the strategy. Since you are using the first letter of each of the listed items to help you create a device that will help you remember, the word FIRST will cue you to look for the first letters of the items whenever you have a list.*

DEFENDS: A WRITING STRATEGY FOR DEFENDING A POSITION

The DEFENDS Writing Strategy was developed by one of the authors of this text (Ellis, 1994). This experimental strategy, designed to be consistent with the principles of SIM strategies, is a demonstration and expression of knowledge strand strategy. DEFENDS has been designed for a student to use to state a position in writing and then provide information that defends that position. This is a common demand encountered on tests and assignments in the secondary school setting. In this strategy the student is taught how to conduct prewriting activities to establish a point of view, list and organize the reasons for taking that position, translate the position and supporting information into writing, and then edit the written product. The steps of DEFENDS are:

D   ecide on audience, goals, and position
E   stimate main ideas and details
F   igure best order of main ideas and details
E   xpress the position in the opening
N   ote each main idea and supporting points
D   rive home the message in the last sentence
S   earch for errors and correct

The mnemonic device DEFENDS is easily recalled by students when their task is to defend a position in writing.

Teaching the DEFENDS Writing Strategy

To teach the DEFENDS Writing Strategy, teachers may say something to their students such as the following:

> In many of your classes, you are given writing assignments. These include reports, book reports, and essay test questions. To perform well on these assignments, you need to state a position and then provide information that effectively explains it. Three processes that can help you perform well on these tasks are to (1) think ahead to consider your goals and to plan and organize your ideas before you begin writing, (2) think during writing to consider how to best express your ideas in a way that will make sense to your audience, and (3) think back to ensure that all of your ideas are clear and free of errors that may distract from your message.
>
> You are going to learn a strategy for explaining your position or ideas in writing. Being able to do this will be beneficial in many ways. First, you will be better able to communicate your knowledge to others. Being able to explain what you know will help others learn about your ideas. Second, this skill will help you meet the requirements of many of your classes. Most reports as well as essay test questions ask you to state a position in writing and then provide information that supports your position. Third, many writing tasks outside of school require you to meet similar requirements. For example, many job applications have spaces where you tell why you want a job and why you think you are qualified.
>
> A well-written essay has at least three major parts: an opening, a body, and a closing. Naturally, the first part is the opening. The first two or three sentences of the opening help your readers to understand your message. They cause readers to activate their own knowledge about a subject and let them know what you are writing about. In other words, they provide an orientation. Consider the opening of the following short essay.

If you like sports, then you probably have a favorite coach. I think the best coach that ever lived is Bear Bryant. He was the head coach for the University of Alabama football team for many years. There are three main reasons why I think "Bear" was the best.

The first reason I think Bear was the best coach is because he won more games than any other coach in NCAA history. The fact that Bear won 323 games during his career is enough for many people to consider him the greatest coach. The original record had been set by Alonzo Stagg many years ago. He won 314 games. It wasn't until 1981 in a game against Auburn that Bear broke the record for most games won. Winning these games was not easy, either. Alabama regularly played tough, nationally ranked teams like Auburn, Georgia, and Tennessee. They also had to beat tough teams like Notre Dame, Miami, and USC.

The second reason is because Baer's teams went to more bowl games than any other team in the history of football. Their favorite bowl game to play was the Sugar Bowl in New Orleans. Bear's teams also played in the Orange Bowl, Peach Bowl, Rose Bowl, and Cotton Bowl, to name a few. He won six national championships at these bowl games.

The third reason I think Bear was the best coach is because he was a great teacher. Bear not only taught the players about football; he also taught them about life. His players learned how to work hard to prepare for tough tasks. They learned how to not give up when things got rough. Most importantly, his players learned the value of teamwork.

Bear used to wear a black and white checkered hat to all of his games. Almost all of his pictures show him wearing the hat. Now, any time I see a hat like that, I think of the greatest coach that ever lived.

The first sentence, "If you like sports, you probably have a favorite coach," caused you to start thinking about sports, and it caused you to think about favorite coaches. In other words, the opening sentence caused you to activate your own background knowledge about sports and coaches. A good opening sentence will do that for the reader. The second sentence, "I think the best coach that ever lived is Bear Bryant," clearly established the position of the writer. There is little doubt about who is the favorite coach of the writer. The next sentence, "There are three main reasons why I think 'Bear' was the best," provided you with an organizational cue. It told you that the writer is getting ready to tell you what the reasons are and then explain them to you. Thus, a good beginning of an essay also establishes the writer's position and cues the reader as to what the essay will be about. An especially good beginning provides the reader organizational cues. For example, the words, "There are three main reasons . . ." cues you to watch for the three reasons as you read on.

The second part of a well-written essay is the middle part, or body. This part provides an explanation for the writer's position. The sentence, "The first reason I think Bear was the best coach is because he won more games than any other coach in NCAA history," is the beginning of the body of the essay.

Notice that the writer used the word "First" to cue the reader that she or he was now beginning to write about the first reason. Also, the writer then clearly stated the reason. The sentences that followed went on to provide supporting details to help explain the reason. When starting to write about the second reason, the author did two things to help readers realize this. She or he started a new paragraph and cued the reader that a second reason was being discussed by using the words "second reason." The writer also did similar things when writing about the third reason, to help you understand the message. Also notice that after stating each reason, the writer explained it using several sentences, or supporting ideas.

The last part of an essay is the closing. The closing is usually a sentence or two that signals the reader that the essay is coming to an end. An especially well-written closing reminds the reader of what the whole essay was about. Notice the last two sentences in the essay about Coach Bryant. They provide a closing for the essay.

To write an essay like this, you need to approach this task in three stages. First, you should "think ahead" to plan your writing. Then you will need to "think during," or as you are writing. Finally, you will need to "think back" to revise and edit your writing. Throughout these processes, you will be asking yourself questions to make sure your ideas will be clear to readers and to think of ways to make it easier for readers to learn as much as possible from you.

To think ahead to plan your writing, there are several things you should think about. One of the most important things to do is to set goals for writing. To set goals, ask yourself, Who will be reading this paper? What do I want them to learn when they read it? What do I want to happen when they read it?

Another important thing to do when planning your essay is to plan your ideas for writing. To plan your ideas, you can use the Organizer Form (see Figure 2.1). First decide what your position will be on a topic. Make sure it takes a particular side, or point of view. Note your position in the box at the top of the form. Next, ask yourself the question, What are the reasons for this position? Each different reason will be a main idea when you write your essay. As you think of different reasons, note them in the boxes labeled "main ideas" on the organizer form. Make sure each reason is different from others already listed. You need a minimum of two different reasons.

Once you have thought of as many different reasons as you can and listed them in the main idea boxes, you need to list specific supporting points for each main idea. To do this, ask yourself the question How can I explain what I mean by this reason? List the supporting points in the small boxes under each main idea. You need to think of as many supporting points as you can, but you need a minimum of three supporting points per main idea.

So far to plan your writing you have set goals, established a position, listed reasons that tell why you have taken that position, and listed supporting points you will use to explain each reason. The ideas you think of first, however, are not necessarily the best ideas to write about first. Now you need to think about the order in which you will present your ideas. To order you main ideas, think about which one of them would be the best to use first when explaining your position. When making this decision, think about who will read your writing and which main idea would help that person best understand your position. Place a 1 in the small box in the corner of the main idea space on your organizer form. That indiates that you will write about this reason first. Order the remaining ideas in a similar way. Figure 2.2 is an organizer form that shows how the main ideas of the Bear Bryant essay were ordered. Once you have decided on the order for presenting your main ideas, repeat this process with each set of supporting points. Make sure that the order is logical.

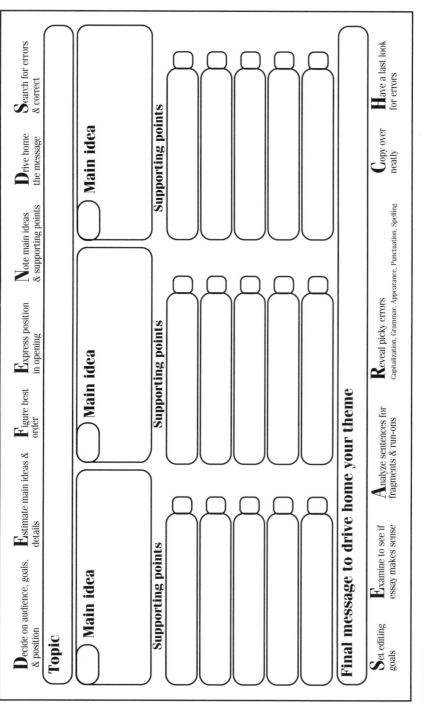

FIGURE 2.1. DEFENDS Organizer Form. From *DEFENDS: A Strategy for Defending a Position in Writing*, by E. Ellis, 1994, unpublished manuscript. Reprinted with permission.

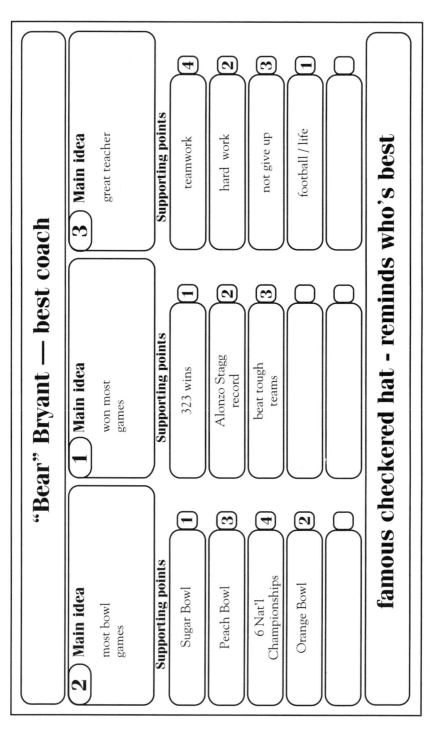

FIGURE 2.2. DEFENDS Organizer Form: Bear Bryant.

Once you have finished planning your essay by noting your position and then listing and ordering your reasons (main ideas) and supporting points, you are ready to write a draft of your paper.

Begin the draft by writing the opening. To write the opening, again think about who may be reading the essay. Ask yourself, What background knowledge will readers probably have that's related to my topic? What will they probably already know about this? What can I say that will get them thinking about my issue? *Then write an opening sentence that activates the thinking about your issue. Next, write a sentence that clearly tells what your position is on this issue. Use the notes you wrote at the top of your organizer form to help you choose the words for this sentence. Make sure it takes a side. Next include a sentence or two in your opening that alerts readers to how your essay is organized. This will help them spot your important points. This can be a simple sentence that tells how many reasons or main ideas will be discussed in the paper.*

After writing your opening, get ready to begin explaining your position in the body of your paper by starting a new paragraph. You will be using the ordered *reasons noted on your planning form to explain your position. First find the reason that you marked 1 and begin the paragraph by stating this reason. A good sentence structure to use is,* The first reason I think that (your position) is because _____. *Then begin explaining your position by writing about the various supporting points you listed earlier under this reason on your organizer form. Be sure to follow the order indicated on your form. A good rule is to write at* least *one sentence for each supporting point you listed on your organizer form. Feel free to add others if you think of them. To get ready to write about each point, ask yourself quesions like* How can I say this in a way that will make it easy for readers to understand my message? *A common mistake some writers make is to say too little about an idea, or not fully explain it. Thus, other good questions to ask yourself include* What else can I say about this to explain it more? *and* What are some examples I can use to help explain this idea? *The intent is to always keep the needs of your readers in mind when you write.*

Once you have finished explaining the first reason for your position, start new paragraphs to explain the other reasons and supporting points. Follow similar procedures as those described above.

When you are ready to write your ending, think again about your readers. Ask yourself, What was the whole essay about? What has my position been on this issue? *Then write a sentence or two that closes the essay. In the closing you need to restate your position in some way. That way, the beginning of your essay states your position, and the ending reaffirms it.*

In the last phase of writing an essay, you need to revise and edit your work. During this phrase you will be asking yourself many questions. Start by setting goals for editing and revising. Ask yourself, Who will be reading this, and what impression do I want them to have of me? *Start checking for possible problems with meaning first. Read your paper out loud, and revise as necessary. Ask yourself questions like* Will this make sense when somebody else reads this part? Will they understand what I mean? Do they know enough about this idea? Is this idea clear, or should I explain it more? Should I reword this sentence to make it easier to understand? Is this sentence too long? Does this idea really belong here or is it too far off from the topic?

You need to also check to make sure you have sufficiently explained your position. Ask questions like Did I establish a position in the opening, maintain that position throughout the paper, and reaffirm it in the closing? Did I include at least two different reasons that tell why I have a particular position? Does each reason have at least three supporting points that explain it?

Finally, you need to check for the types of errors that distract from your message. Questions to ask include Are there any words that are misspelled? Does every sentence begin with a capital letter? Did I capitalize the first letters of proper names? Have I used capital letters where they do not belong? Are sentences punctuated correctly? Do verbs and nouns match in terms of plurals and tenses? Any word omissions?

Once you have finished revising and editing your work, you need to recopy it to make it neat, clean, and free of errors. The very last thing to do is ask yourself, Did I meet my goals?

The remembering system DEFENDS has been designed to assist the student in remembering this strategy. The student must understand the process described above before the remembering system becomes useful. Once the student has been introduced to the remembering system, the student must learn how to associate the remembering system with the strategy and to the outcomes that are to be achieved by using the strategy. An association for the DEFENDS Strategy is:

> To help you remember to use DEFENDS when you write, think of what the word defends means. Defend is what you do when you are explaining how you feel about something—you are defending a position. You will think of the word defends whenever you have writing assignments that call for your position. That will be how you cue yourself to explain your position using DEFENDS.

Using Organizers

GOAL: To develop and implement advance organizers, lesson organizers, and post organizers to promote students' strategy acquisition and generalization.

ORIENTATION

Disorganized information is difficult to learn and remember. Well-organized information is just as difficult to learn and remember if the organization is not clear to the learner. Take, for example, a lesson on the construction of the periodic table of the elements. To understand its construction, students need to understand the traditional column matrix and the groupings of elements by type. This is in addition to comprehending concepts such as element, metals, and carbon. Although we might assume the information is well organized for the student by the periodic table's structure, we need to remember that both the content and that type of structure (i.e., the column matrix) may be foreign to students. In many instances, texts and class discussions are as potentially unclear to students as the periodic table; they can be clear only to those familiar with the content or organizational structure.

When the organization of content is apparent, learning and recall are enhanced (Salomon, 1981). For example, when the information in a reading is clearly organized, or its organization is described in advance, comprehension is improved (Meyer, Brandt, & Bluth, 1980; Taylor & Beach, 1984). This same principle of organization applies to the classroom teaching of content or procedures. When organization is made explicit, learning is improved. By providing organizers as part of their teaching, teachers can enhance comprehension of both distinct units of information and their relationships. Examples of organizers commonly used in teaching include semantic maps or webs (e.g., Bos & Anders, 1990), think sheets (Englert, Raphael, Anderson, Anthony, & Stevens, 1991), lesson organizers (Lenz, Marrs, Schumaker, & Deshler, 1993), and lesson outlines or syllabi. *Organizer* is a widely used term that describes a device for depicting organization. It can be any of a number of graphic devices (e.g., Crank & Bulgren, 1993) or a nonvisual (e.g., discussed) part of learning activities. See Crank and Bulgren (1993) for sample graphic organizer devices. Not all organizers are created equal, however. They can take many different forms and can be used at different stages of the lesson. The teacher must make decisions as to which type of organizer is best to use and when. This decision should be based on such factors as clarity of the organizer, density of content, use of the organizer (e.g., will students have to reproduce or complete it?), how accurately it represents its contents' organization, and whether when it is used it enhances or detracts from the presentation of the content.

Interest in the value of organizers in teaching was initially centered on the use of "advance organizers" (e.g., Ausubel, 1960; Ausubel, Novak, & Hanesian, 1968). Ausubel described advance organizers as tools to "provide ideational scaffolding for the stable incorporation and retention of more detailed and differentiated material that follows" (1968, p. 148). As part of instruction, an advance organizer can be a teaching process to both introduce and initiate learning of a given topic. Thus, as a teaching practice, *advance organizer* is operationally defined as follows: An instructional *routine* preceding learning that serves to overview the organization and integration of to-be-learned information. Advance organizers are most likely to be useful to promote learning when students do not have adequate background knowledge for performing a particular task, do not make connections between prior knowledge and to-be-learned information, and/or do not recognize relationships among to-be-learned information.

Organizers also may be beneficial at times other than at the beginning of lessons. A *post organizer* is an instructional *routine* following learning that (a) confirms the organization and integration of learned information; (b) forecasts application of the learned information; and (c) forecasts the goals, organization, and integration of future related learning. Post organizers may serve to revisit the advance organizer, to review and update it, or to summarize a lesson and predict future lessons.

A *lesson organizer* is an instructional *device* that serves to refocus student attention on organization and promote integration of information as it is learned. It differs from advance and post organizers in that it is a device and not an instructional routine that may incorporate a device. The device may be the same type as those used during advance and post organizers (see Figure 3.1). The teacher might use the lesson organizer to emphasize key parts of a lesson (e.g., each time a new vocabulary term is introduced) or to point out to students how different activities in that day's class relate (e.g., reviewing how to identify the main idea of a paragraph and listening to a partner state a main idea).

Although the advance organizer enjoys the most empirical evidence supporting its use, studies (e.g., Lenz, 1983) have indicated that lesson organizers and post organizers have value as well. The desired contributions to learning are most likely to be achieved when an advance organizer is combined with appropriate use of lesson and post organizers. Data that evaluate student learning when organizers are used are limited, however, because it appears that few organizers of any type are used in educational settings (Lenz, Alley, & Schumaker, 1987).

While research on the use of organizers indicates that they generally contribute to learning, research specifically on use of organizers with students with learning disabilities (LD) indicates that they are sometimes ineffective. Mere exposure to organizers is not effective in the case of individuals, such as those with LD, who do not (a) independently recognize advance organizers when they are used by teachers (Lenz et al., 1987), (b) independently use lesson organizers to organize learning in their notes (Scanlon, Schumaker, & Deshler, 1995), or (c) independently take advantage of reviews incorporating post organizers at the end of a lesson. When students with LD are made aware of organizers and are prompted to become actively involved in using them, however, their learning appears to improve (e.g., Lenz et al., 1987; Scanlon, Duran, Reyes, & Gallego, 1991; Scanlon, Schumaker, & Deshler, 1994).

The model of instruction described in this section focuses on the use and integration of advance organizers, lesson organizers, and post organizers through active student involvement. The model is based on the

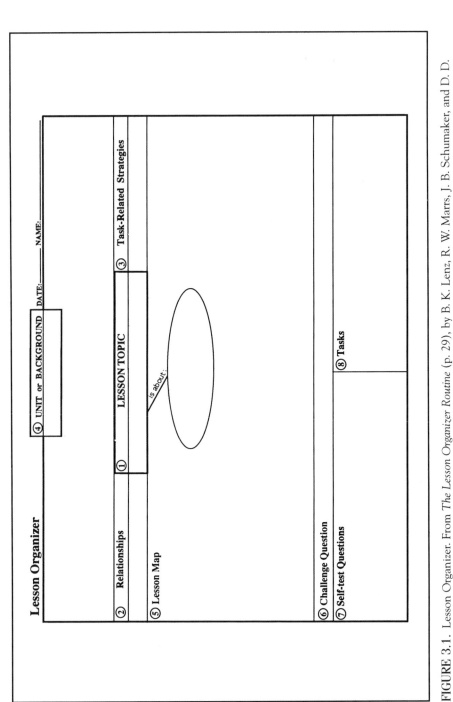

FIGURE 3.1. Lesson Organizer. From *The Lesson Organizer Routine* (p. 29), by B. K. Lenz, R. W. Marrs, J. B. Schumaker, and D. D. Deshler. Copyright 1993 by Lenz, Marrs, Schumaker, and Deshler. Reprinted with permission. Deshler, 1993, Lawrence, KS: Edge Enterprises.

authors' and their colleagues' research involving students with LD. Although, all three organizers ideally would be incorporated into a lesson, using only one or two of the organizers is preferable to using none.

PREPARATION

Organizers require preparation. If you do not know the content or activity for a lesson well or if it has been a while since you have taught a particular lesson, then you should prepare you organizers after you have learned or reviewed the content. Organizers should promote organization and integration beyond what is included in a manual, textbook, typical worksheet, or practice activity. The organizer accurately reflects both the content of the lesson and your plan for teaching it. Once you have developed the framework for your organizer (a graphic device or outline of a discussion), you can use that framework each time you teach its particular content.

TIME CONSIDERATIONS

The goal of instruction determines the length and type of organizer that is required. In general, an advance organizer used to introduce a lesson should take no more than a few minutes. Organizers within a lesson used to bridge ideas and concepts and to illustrate relationships and lesson structure may be revisited several times during a lesson for as short as 1 minute each time, and post organizers used to summarize a lesson can take no more than 5 minutes. Each of these time estimates assumes the teacher will present the organizer to students with minimal student input; this is the most time efficient but not always the ideal scenario for engaging students. Ideally, students will be actively involved in reviewing organizers and even constructing them. Time spent on organizers can be lengthened when a new phase of instruction or unit is being introduced or when students are not seeing the relationships among lesson content. Organizers, therefore, must be conceptualized as an instructional tool, their use to be expanded or condensed depending on the background knowledge of students and their attempts to make information meaningful. Procedures for teaching with each type of organizer follow.

PROCEDURES
Advance Organizers

1. *Familiarize students with the concept of an advance organizer.* Because advance organizers are not a routine part of most lessons students experience and when used their purpose is not always stressed, students may not understand them without a little advance explanation. This familiarization can involve the students by asking them some probing questions, the answers to which will define and explain the use of advance organizers. As students become familiar with the use of organizers, this discussion can be phased out. The following is an example of such a discussion:

> *What does the word* organize *mean? Yes, to* organize *is to put things together in some logical order. What are some examples of things you can organize? [Solicit ideas.] Now, what does the word* advance *mean? That's right, to come before. So if we organize in advance, when are we doing it? [Solicit answers.] Good; an organizer is something that shows you how things are organized. Examples include the table of contents in a book, the game plan drawn up by a football team, and a family tree that shows how all of your relatives are related. So, if we are going to have an advance organizer for today's lesson, what do you think that will be? [Solicit answers.] Yes, an advance organizer is something that shows you how the lesson is organized before we begin it.*
>
> *What are some of the reasons we would want to know how a lesson is organized before we begin it? [Solicit answers such as so we will know what is to be covered, what we already know that is relevant to the topic, and what to listen/watch for, and so we will better understand how the content of the lesson fits together.]*

Once students have become familiar with the concept of advance organizers, you may begin future lessons with step 2.

2. *Gain attention and cue use of organizer.* Inform students that you are ready to begin class and inform them that you are going to provide an advance organizer that they are going to be involved in constructing. (You can merely present organizers while students watch, but they are far more effective when students are actively involved in the presentation.) It is a good idea to cue students to copy the organizer into their notes or at a minimum to jot down some notes about the organizer. Depending on the complexity of the organizer (and the note-taking abilities of your students), you may distribute skeletal organizers that include the structure but no content (see Figure 3.2). Fully completed organizers can be handed out, but students may not attend to them while you are leading a presentation of them.

Initially, and periodically during the course of the year, you should ask students to define an advance organizer and explain how an organizer can help them to learn.

What is an organizer? That's right, an organizer is information provided before, during, or after learning that helps us understand (a) how what we are learning relates to what we know, (b) how information is organized for learning, (c) why and how we are supposed to learn something, and (d) what is most important for us to know. What is an advance organizer? Yes, it is an organizer presented before a lesson begins.

Gradually, students should be taught to automatically identify and use organizers to enhance their learning, without teacher prompts. You as the teacher merely prompt and guide students to generate the organizer content. If lesson time permits, you may encourage students to design the organizer. Over time you may find that you can even turn over the responsibility of initiating lesson and post organizers to students. Your role then would become one of monitoring the accuracy of the proposed organizer and then confirming, clarifying, and elaborating on what students have generated.

Where do we begin today? Good, we start with an organizer. What did we cover yesterday? Right, so what are we going to cover today? Okay, let's write that on the chalkboard, and let me add two more topics that we will get to today. Okay, what's next?

3. *Review previous learning.* The next step of teaching with the advance organizer is usually to review information that has already been covered and learned. Ask your students to tell you what they studied in the last lesson (e.g., topics and subtopics); then ask them what they learned (e.g., conclusions, concepts, ideas, results, consequences).

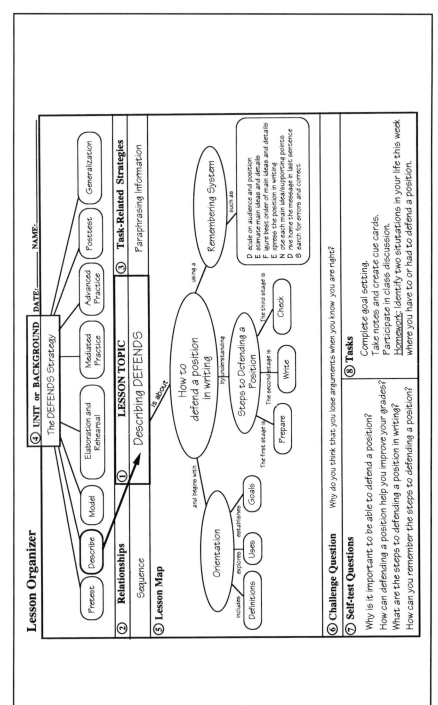

FIGURE 3.2. Sample Advance Organizer for a DEFENDS lesson.

What did we cover yesterday? Right, we learned about the steps in the DEFENDS Writing Strategy. [Write "DEFENDS Strategy" on the top and center of the chalkboard, and draw a box around it.] How many steps are in the DEFENDS Writing Strategy? Good, there are seven major steps that help us to remember the strategy. [Draw seven boxes horizontally underneath the box labeled "DEFENDS Strategy."] Okay, what are the seven steps that we use to cue us to remember what to do? Right. [Write one step in each of the seven boxes.] Okay, we have written the first step in the first box; how do we do this step? [Elicit the characteristics and explanations for this step and list them below the first box. Repeat this process for each of the steps in the strategy.]

Conclude this step of using the advance organizer by relating what was covered in the last lesson to the overall purpose of the lesson (i.e., learning the DEFENDS Writing Strategy).

4. *Identify topics and goals.* Ask students to identify what the lesson topic or goal is for the day. The goal may be related to understanding the strategy via teacher modeling of the strategy, or the goal may be to continue to practice the strategy and reach the mastery criterion.

What are we going to do today? That's right, we are going to learn how to practice defending a position when writing. [Identify ways you are going to practice and add them to the advance organizer as you discuss them.] We are going to discuss how to plan and organize your ideas. [Add this to the organizer.] Then we will think as we write to be sure we express our ideas clearly. [Write this on the organizer.] And, finally, we are each going to check back for clarity and errors. [Add to the organizer.]

If the lesson follows a procedure routinely used in your class (e.g., learning a strategy, preparing to interview an expert from the community on the lesson's topic), students should be able to help predict what activities will be written on the organizer, including knowing in what order they will occur.

5. *Define content.* Once the goal of the lesson has been established, the content or the concepts that are to be learned should be presented. This is easier for some stages of strategy learning than others. The content refers to what the student is going to learn about the strategy during that particular instructional stage. While the steps of the strategy are first presented in the Describe stage of the instructional process, each of the other stages promotes a different level of understanding related to the strategy. The following is a list of the content features of each instructional stage that should appear on the advance organizer for a corresponding strategy lesson.

- Pretest and obtain a commitment to learn: Understand the need for the strategy.

- Describe: Understand the steps of the strategy and the processes related to each step.

- Model: Understand how to think about and perform each step and learn how to think aloud.

- Verbal elaboration and rehearsal: Understand the meaning of each step and memorize the strategy steps and all of their processes.

- Controlled practice: Learn to use (practice) the strategy by applying it to content and situations for which its use is relatively easy.

- Advanced practice: Understand the application of the strategy under increasingly difficult situations, such as those encountered on a near-daily basis.

- Posttest and obtain a commitment to generalize: Understand that the strategy has been mastered and can be used to enhance learning in other contexts. Encourage the student to identify reasons to want to continue to use the strategy in the same and other contexts.

- Generalization: Understand the application and adaptation process for the expanded application of the strategy.

The definition of the content of each stage should include what the student will learn, an explanation of the content, and a discussion or review of key vocabulary that might be required. Notice in the example that follows how much the teacher elicits the content from the students. Again, as students learn to expect to use advance organizers, they well become more able to participate in generating organizer information.

What is a model? That's partially correct; can someone add to what we mean by a model? How will the model that I lend help you to learn the strategy? Good, you will better understand what to do and how to think through each step and all of its parts. Why am I also going to have you model the strategy? That's right. It will give us a chance to see if you have the right idea about how to think about the strategy.

6. *Personalize learning.* Learning is personalized through the use of carefully constructed rationales and examples of success in learning. The purpose is to contribute to the motivation of the student; rationales alone, however, cannot motivate the student. A rationale is constructed through the following process:

Step 1: Construct a general and positive if–then statement that is related to the strategy and the specific instructional stage. The if–then statement should portray a positive cause and effect relationship.

If you learn to generalize the DEFENDS Writing Strategy to use in your other subjects, then it is more likely that you are going to write better papers and get better grades on these papers.

Step 2: Construct another positive if–then statement in which the "if" part of the rationale is more short-term, specific, and personalized, but still believable. Leave the "then" portion of the rationale open for the students to complete.

If you had used the DEFENDS Writing Strategy on the history assignment last night, then what might have happened?

Step 3: Construct another positive if–then statement in which the "if" portion of the statement is general and you allow the student to generate more specific information about benefits.

If you begin generalizing the DEFENDS Writing Strategy, then what might happen in some of your classes?

Step 4: Continue to construct if–then statements eliciting student assistance. Incorporate a few negative if–then statements. A negative if–then statement focuses on the consequences of not learning or applying the strategy.

If you only use this strategy when you are in this class, then what's likely to happen in your other classes? That's right, your efforts in other classes will probably not pay off as well.

Rationales and examples should be sprinkled throughout the instructional process. As instruction in a strategy progresses, the responsibility for generating rationales and examples should be shifted to the student. In fact, as the student sees the benefits of the strategy, it is a nice motivational twist to encourage the student to become an advocate of the strategy by having her or him provide rationales to other students and to challenge the student to justify spending time teaching the strategy to others.

7. *Identify expectations.* Once the content of a lesson has been clearly identified, the next step is to outline how the lesson will be achieved. You should inform students of the activities in which they will be engaged (e.g., modeling, group work, discussion) and what type for performance you will expect. You also need to identify what you will be doing so that they will know what to expect of you.

> *We are going to spend about 20 minutes practicing as a group. I will lead the practice and ask you to volunteer to help me out. Everyone will need to get at least three or four chances to help me out. Then you will work independently for the rest of the period. I will be walking around the room to check on you while you are working. Okay, let's begin the group review.*

Reading through this 7-step procedure may give the impression that it is a lengthy process taking far more than "a few minutes." You will find that these discussions go quickly and lead one right into the next. You do not need to dwell on each point; this is simply to introduce the lesson.

Lesson Organizers

1. *Cue organization.* Students will profit more from the advance organizer you presented at the beginning of the lesson if you refer to the organization it cued throughout the rest of the lesson. This may be done as simply as by using organizing words such as "first," "second," and "third" as you talk. You may also list the topics on the chalkboard as they are covered or, more ideally, if you have already presented an organizational framework in a graphic, outline, or study guide form, point and refer to that framework as you go through the lesson.

Hopefully, you have selected to begin the lesson with an advance organizer. If for some reason you have not, it is never too late. Use these lesson organizer steps as you progress through the lesson.

*There are three parts to this step. The first part of this step includes
. . . [point]. The second part of this step includes . . . . What have we
covered so far in the strategy? What is the next step?*

2. *Cue important content.* The goals of the lesson are more likely to be achieved when you clearly distinguish between helpful information and critical information. This can be accomplished by repeating critical information or highlighting it by circling or marking it on the chalkboard or overhead projector. Students who have not been taught strategies to take notes are likely to take notes only when information has been written on the chalkboard or an overhead transparency.

*This is very important information. Let's go over it again. Be sure to
take notes on this. Write this down. Do you think that this is something that is important? What are the most important bits of information for you to remember at this point?*

3. *Cue relationships.* The primary purpose of an organizer is to represent the integration of information. For this reason, it is essential that more than just the content of the organizer be emphasized. The relationships among content must all be considered. Typically, students and teachers are oriented more toward the "facts" than toward the relationships among them. It is not uncommon for a class to review a graphic organizer, never once discussing how the content is organized or the nature of the relationships depicted. But if it were not for the relationships, an organizer would only be a scattered collection of information.

You cue relationships by distinguishing links between and among ideas and concepts. One way you can link ideas is through association. When you cue relationships through association, you are trying to link something that is currently happening to something that the student already knows.

*Yesterday we talked about another type of writing error that you were
making when you organized your content. Can you remember what
that error was? What did you decide you should do about it? Right.*

Now let's look at the error that you are making right now. What do you think you should do in this case?

Another way to link information is via graphics. Boxes illustrating components of the lesson or of a concept can be linked with lines to indicate which ideas are related. Larger boxes or circles can be used to group several components together to show how different parts of the strategy are related (see Figure 3.3).

Look at the first three steps of this strategy. In these steps you are preparing to write. I'm going to draw a circle around these steps and write the word "preparing" in the column to indicate that it is a primary task. Now, look at the next three steps. What are you going to be doing across these steps? Good, you are going to be writing down information. I am going to put a circle around these three steps and label this circle "writing." Now, what is involved in the last step? Sure, you're going to be checking your work. Let's put a circle around this step and label it "checking." Notice that these three circles are written in the order that they happen: preparing, writing, and checking.

4. *Cue expectations.* As instruction proceeds, it is helpful to continually remind students of the instructional goals, mastery requirements, and actions they should be engaged in.

I expect you to reach mastery today. I expect you to know these steps and what each step means. Do you need to know these? How many paragraphs do you need to write? What are you supposed to do now?

5. *Cue self-check.* As the lesson progresses, refer students back to the content covered on the organizer so far. They can use this time to be sure they have properly understood the organizer and to make certain they fully understand the content being covered before the lesson goes on.

Post Organizers

1. *Gain attention, cue organizer.* The first step in delivering the post organizer is to announce that it is time to use the post organizer to review or "get closure." As with the advance organizer, you can gradually shift

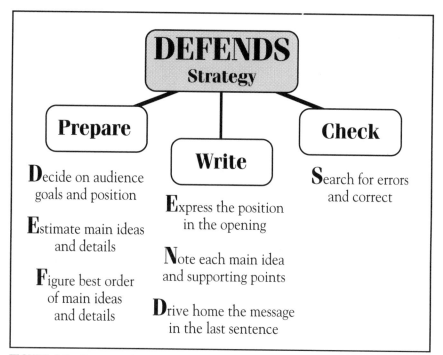

FIGURE 3.3. Organizer for DEFENDS.

the responsibility for generating post organizers to students as they become more aware of the purposes of organizers and how to structure them.

Let's wrap up today's lesson by reviewing what we learned.

2. *Evaluate acquisition.* The evaluation should be structured to provide information to both the teacher and the student. Evaluations can be oral or written. If the goal of the lesson is related to understanding or remembering the strategy steps, for example, the evaluation could consist of a round of comprehension and recall questions asking students to name and explain the steps. If the evaluation is of strategy procedures, students could describe their process or turn in a product that indicates they followed procedures (e.g., a self-selected representative paragraph). Also, evaluation at the end of a practice session could be based on "what if" questions based on the problems and feedback from practice examples.

If you don't have time to write down all the things that you think should be written down, what should you do?

3. *Evaluate integration.* If you have used a graphic device during instruction, put the framework on the chalkboard with student input or distribute copies to students for them to fill out. This is an excellent way to determine whether they understand the relationships among information in the lesson. Less effective but still useful is to present the organization to the students one more time. Ask students to explain how information covered from previous lessons fits with the current lesson. This is especially important in strategies instruction because each instructional stage is built on information acquired in the previous instructional stage.

4. *Forecast generalization.* Throughout the instructional process it is important to discuss how the strategy can be used across settings and situations. When you forecast generalization, you are informing and asking students as to where and when they can use the strategy. Ask for rationales for using the strategy and have students discuss example situations at home, at work, and in the community, as well as situations they might encounter in various classroom settings.

5. *Communicate results.* Inform students as to whether the goals have been met. Allow students to be part of the monitoring process. If the goal was to completely memorize all the strategy steps and the goal was not met, then students should be aware of this. A progress chart on which each student can mark progress on a daily basis is useful in prompting student awareness of where they are in the instructional process.

6. *Forecast learning.* Finally, tell your students what the goal for the next lesson will be. In time, they will become aware of the strategy learning process, and you can allow them to project what the next step will be.

Tomorrow you are all going to take the posttest for the strategy. I will give you some time to review the strategy and practice it on your own before we begin the posttest. Once we get through the posttest, we will start talking about generalizing the strategy to your other classes.

Also, continually remind your students that future success will come only when both the strategy and their efforts are applied together.

Before the bell rings, I have something to tell you. We have been working on this strategy for a week now. You are all doing a fine job. But remember, the strategy is not magic. The strategy is merely a tool that you have to learn to use. Your effort is also very important. I know that when you learn this strategy and combine it with your effort, you are going to be more successful in your classes. Why is that? [Solicit responses.]

ENHANCING INSTRUCTION AND MOTIVATION

The goals associated with the use of organizers may not be achieved if the delivery becomes regimented and unexciting. Organizers are for daily use across all instructional lessons. As a result, the potential for dullness increases. Yet students should be taught to expect to use organizers, participate in generating them, and use them to enhance learning. Sufficient variety must be infused in the use of organizers so that student interest is maintained. The following are some novel methods for implementing organizers. A variety of these methods, combined with straightforward use of organizers, can significantly enhance student interest, participation, and learning.

1. At the beginning of class, organize students into groups. Give them time to review what was learned from the previous lesson. If the previous day was related to practice, return their previous day's work and have them discuss the types of mistakes they learned and how they might correct them. Have each group report its findings to the class.

2. Have students design an organizer with boxes and lines showing the major parts of the strategy and what is involved in each part.

3. During an organizer activity, assign one student to be responsible for remembering what was first, another student what was second, and so forth. Periodically, return to students and ask, "What was the first thing we need to do . . . what was the second . . . the third . . .?"

4. During a post organizer, instead of asking review questions yourself, let the students ask each other the review questions. As each asks a question, the person answering should tell whether the question was a good review question (i.e., consistent with the goals or major points in the lesson) and then answer the question. Have students refer to an organizer to support their point.

INSTRUCTIONAL DECISIONS

Organizers are used to clarify the organization and integration of information. They should be infused throughout the instructional process. In fact, every instructional activity in the SIM should be enhanced with the use of organizers. Evaluate the effects of organizers by asking students to identify the organization of information and the relationships among information and activities. The benefits of the use of organizers are going to be most observable over time, that is, once students begin to understand their construction and use.

TROUBLESHOOTING

If students do not see the benefits of using organizers and ignore cues to take notes or participate in discussions, you may want to try using outlines or study guides to prompt their attention to organization. Outlines and study guides are a type of organizer; however, they do not prompt as much independence. Begin with study guides that provide a lot of detail. Gradually provide study guides that have less detail and require the student to fill in the information. The student should be prompted to ask questions that relate to the missing information.

Challenge to the reader: Develop a post organizer that summarizes the key contents (and their relationships) of this chapter. After you have made your organizer, compare it to the one in Appendix B.

Providing Effective Feedback

GOAL: To provide students with information about strategy performance that results in improved performance, leading to increased independence.

ORIENTATION

As students begin to practice performing a strategy independently, they will need feedback to understand what they are doing that is effective and what behaviors need to be changed or improved. While we all learn from experience and practice, effective feedback guides us to be efficient and effective learners. Effective feedback is both positive and corrective. There are some specific things you can do to enhance the effectiveness of the feedback you provide.

PREPARATION

Because each strategy comprises a set of behaviors students should perform, you can prepare a performance checklist of these behaviors. As you gain experience teaching the strategy, you will probably find that there is also a set of errors students commonly commit when performing the strategy. A performance checklist contains a way to record whether students are performing correct behaviors, and it allows you to maintain a record of incorrect behaviors. Although such a checklist may seem unnecessary for giving immediate feedback, it will be very useful for tracking feedback (and students' strategy performance) over time.

PROCEDURES

The following is an overview of research findings concerning effective feedback.

1. *Feedback should include praise and information on what was done right.*

2. *Feedback should focus on correct behaviors as well as identify errors.* Unfortunately, the feedback teachers most often provide tends to be either too global for students to clearly understand the problem, or non-explicit (e.g., merely identifying the error). More effective feedback focuses the student's attention on the types of behaviors correctly performed, as well as types of errors made and how to avoid them (Howell, 1986; Kea, 1987; Kline, 1989). Consider the following examples, which illustrate this point.

PROBLEM

When practicing the DEFENDS Writing Strategy, Vince frequently provides closing statements that introduce a new topic.

Example of Feedback That Is Too Global

TEACHER: It looks like you are consistently doing a good job of identifying important details to support your position, but you need to work on your closing statements.

Example of Feedback That Focuses Only on Specific Errors

TEACHER: You start out by clearly stating that you believe punk rock was a reaction to the soft-rock and disco movements of the 1970s. You provide examples of how punk songs mock those two styles; you even provide quotes from Sid Vicious and Johnny Rotten. But then when we get to your conclusion you state that rap music is a response to alternative rock and dance music. You have not provided the reader with a summary of your argument, and you have introduced a new topic but provided no supporting points.

Example of Feedback Focusing on the Types of Correct Behaviors and Error Types

TEACHER: Your writing is much better since you began using DEFENDS. Your progress chart shows your improvement, but you still need to improve your scores. Let's look at your latest score sheet because it is a good example of what you need to work on. As you can see, your opening statement and supporting points are all well organized and well stated. I particularly like the way you stated when an idea was your own or a punk rocker's. See where you lost points though? Yes, your closing statement; and look at what's checked. It does not restate your position. Why should it do that? How could you state your closing?

3. *Feedback on strategy performance should be relative to an established mastery criteria.* Students perform a strategy better when (a) expectations for performance are clear to them and (b) they know how their performance will be evaluated. Feedback, therefore, should be relative to a mastery criteria. In other words, students should understand both how well they need to be able to perform specific strategic behaviors and how close they are to performing at that level. Two useful devices for demonstrating the relation of actual performance to mastery criteria are checklists and charts or graphs.

4. *Use performance checklists to enhance the clarity of feedback.* Using performance checklists can greatly increase your ability to provide explicit feedback because you will not have to rely on your memory. It also allows you to quickly determine the most common types of errors students are making. Figure 4.1 illustrates a performance score sheet that can be used to evaluate a student's writing sample when using the DEFENDS Writing Strategy. This sheet can be used to quickly record whether the strategy is used appropriately or, when not, what the problem is. Note that the same sheet can be used to assign the student's sample a score. The most common errors students make can be easily indicated on the sheet. Forms such as this can be used by both teachers and students to check progress toward mastery.

Checklists of common errors are particularly desirable when students are performing strategies that do not produce permanent products. They allow you to record the behavior as the student is performing the strategy. They also allow you to provide specific feedback without interrupting the student in mid-performance. Checklists should not be limited to cataloging errors; remember, effective feedback includes explicit information

DEFENDS Writing Strategy Score Sheet

NAME _____

CONTENT SCORE

POSITION STATEMENTS

Opening statement   0   2

Closing statement   0   2

Problem areas

____ Opening statement does not clearly show an exact position

____ Change in position in text error

____ Closing sentence does not restate position

____ Wording in closing sentence too similar to opening sentence

REASONS

1st reason   0   2

2nd reason   0   2

Problem areas

____ Only one reason provided

____ Reasons not different

____ No reasons

ELABORATIONS / DETAILS

of 1st reason's elaborations _____

# of 2nd reason's elaborations _____

# of additional elaborations _____

TOPIC _____

Computing CONTENT Score

Total Positions Score _____

Total Reasons Score _____

Total Elaborations _____

+ [ ]

CONTENT Score

Minimum score for mastery = 14

MECHANICS SCORE

	1	2	3	4	5	6	7	8	9	10	11	12	13	14	15	16	17	18	19	20	Category Totals
Sentence																					
Paragraph																					
Capitalization																					
Punctuation																					
Spelling																					
Other																					

Error Codes

SENTENCE Errors

F = Fragment
RO = Run-on
IL = Illogical

PARAGRAPH Errors

R = Relationship error
PV = Point-of-view error
T = Tense error
S = Sequence error

Computing MECHANICS Score

Total # of errors = [ ]

Total # of words = [ ]

= [ ]

MECHANICS Score

Mastery = less than .05 errors per word

Total Errors

FIGURE 4.1. DEFENDS Writing Strategy Performance Score Sheet.

on what was done right. At the teacher's discretion, the checklist can be shared with the student or simply used as a referent when formulating feedback.

5. *Feedback on strategy performance presented in chart (or graph) form can readily identify progress toward mastery.* If you provide students with charts that allow them to record their performance scores, you will probably find that most of your students are consistently more motivated to master the strategy. The charts should have the mastery criteria indicated on them so that students can view their progress toward mastery and ascertain how close they are to performing at mastery levels. Figure 4.2 is an example of a student's progress chart. Notice how the mastery criteria for content and mechanics are indicated on the chart. Plotting performance is particularly meaningful to students when they complete the chart. Remember, effective feedback tells students not only what scores they earned but also how they earned them.

6. *Effective feedback includes student elaboration.* By asking students to discuss the feedback shared with them, you may gain an understanding of both how well they understood the feedback and their conceptualization of the task (Adelman & Taylor, 1983). In discussions with students you may realize their errors are based on a misconception of the task (e.g., Vince's belief that the closing statement should introduce the reader to a "next" topic to consider). This is information you may not deduce by preparing to give feedback without input from the student.

Providing students with opportunities to elaborate using their own language during feedback can be an effective technique. The degree of coaching necessary for student elaboration depends on the individual student's experience with elaboration and the nature of any language disability she or he may have. Consider the following dialogue for an example.

PROBLEM

Violet is not effectively monitoring spelling errors when using The Paragraph Writing Strategy (Schumaker & Lyerla, 1991), an expository writing strategy.

Example Illustrating Failure to Cue Student Elaboration of the Feedback

TEACHER: You need to focus more on finding and correcting spelling errors. You can use a "secretary's speller" to find hard-to-spell words. Okay, let's give it a shot.

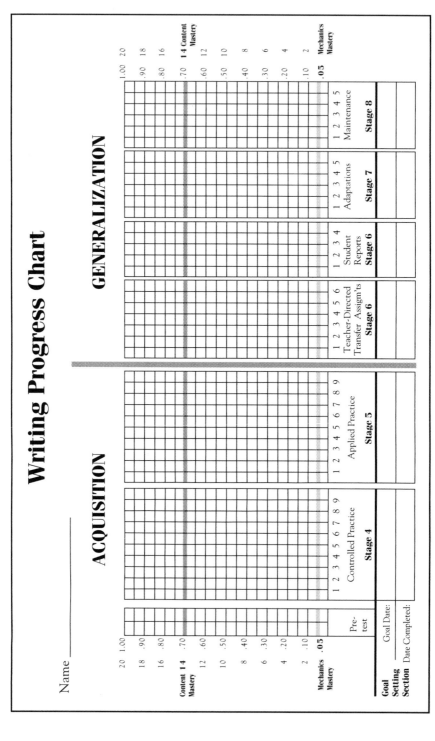

FIGURE 4.2. DEFENDS Writing Strategy Progress Chart.

Example Illustrating Feedback That Cues Student Elaboration

TEACHER: We've talked about the need to focus more on finding and correcting spelling errors, and we've talked before about using a "secretary's speller" to find hard-to-spell words. Now, let's say you've just written your essay and you're now ready to go back and edit it. Using the speller, explain to me how you will use it.

VIOLET: Well, I'm going to look over my writing and mark the words I'm not sure are spelled right. Then I'm going to look them up in the speller.

TEACHER: How will you be able to find them using the speller?

VIOLET: The speller has the words spelled like they sound with the correct spelling next to the word. I can find it by its sound. You know. The way the letters sound.

TEACHER: Okay. Let's give it a shot. Please show me how you will do it.

7. *Effective feedback focuses on increasing effort to use a strategy.* Ultimately, students should believe that their successes at completing specific tasks are due in large part to their efforts at using the best strategies for approaching tasks. Likewise, they should recognize that their less-than-successful experiences at task completion are due in large part to the use of less effective strategies (e.g., trying to identify and organize thoughts, express them in writing, and edit errors simultaneously). Feedback provides an excellent opportunity for addressing such beliefs. Two approaches you may wish to use are (a) effort focusing and (b) attribution retraining.

Effort focusing refers to the frequent, if not constant, reference to the role that effort plays in success. The role of effort can be addressed both indirectly and directly. Indirect references to the role effort plays in success occur in the daily dialogue teachers have with students. These dialogues are not necessarily related to the academic tasks on which students are working. The following are some examples.

- Commenting on others' use of effort in relation to success:
  - "I noticed that the team won again. It must be tough with so many key players who are hurt and can't play. The team must really be trying hard to use a good strategy for winning the game."

- "It must take a lot of effort for that student to do so well. I know for a fact that that's a tough class. I know some students who didn't try as hard, and you can guess what happened to them."

- "It was hard for her, but she kept trying to use an effective strategy until she got it. If she hadn't tried so hard, she would never have done as well."

- Commenting on personal effort in relation to success:

  - "Losing weight is really hard for me. This diet is a killer. It's working because I'm really trying to make it work. Last time I was on a diet, I didn't try to stick with it. I wasn't trying to use a good self-control strategy."

Direct references to the role that effort plays in success occur in the daily dialogue teachers have with students. They are typically related to the academic tasks on which students are working. The following are some examples.

- Commenting on student's effort in relation to past success:

  - "This procedure is hard to learn. You seem to be really working on getting it. Keep trying; you're starting to get it."

  - "What is most significant about this work is the effort you put into it."

- Commenting on student's effort in relation to future success:

  - "So where are you going to focus your effort next time?"

  - "From now on, try putting a lot more of your effort into doing this part of the strategy."

  - "To be successful at doing this, focus your efforts on . . ."

  - "If you didn't try as hard when doing this strategy, what part do you think would suffer most?"

  - "What is the easiest part of this strategy? On what part do you have to try hardest?"

Attribution retraining refers to a procedure used to help change students' beliefs about who is in control of success. Many students with mild disabilities tend to attribute their success to factors beyond personal control (e.g., "I was lucky—this assignment was easy") instead of their own positive attributes (e.g., "I'm good at doing this"; "I'm really trying to use this in the best way"); also, they attribute failure to personal attributes (e.g., "I'm dumb"; "I'm no good at this"; "I can't learn this") (Mehring & Colson, 1990). These beliefs about self and success run counter to the overall philosophy of strategy instruction—independent functioning and personal responsibility for actions (Ellis, 1985). Changing these beliefs about responsibility for success is every bit as important as teaching students strategies.

Teaching students to make positive attributions regarding success and failure can have a positive impact on learning (see Litch & Kistner, 1986). Giving feedback is an ideal time to incorporate this attribution training. What you want students to believe is that success is due largely to efforts at using the best strategy for the task and that failure is due to persistence in using a less effective strategy. Students should also know that when they make errors it is a part of the learning process and not their fate for life. Feedback, therefore, should focus on the role that effort at using the best strategy plays in success. To elicit these more positive attributions from students, the teacher can make the positive attribution for the student and then solicit acknowledgment, ask students to choose between two attributions (a positive and a negative), or simply cue the student to make a positive attribution. The following dialogues illustrate these practices.

- Teacher makes positive attribution for student and cues student acknowledgment:

  TEACHER: Judging by this work, it looks like you are really trying to use that expository writing strategy. Is that right John?

  JOHN: Yeah, I am.

- Teacher provides students with choices between positive and counterproductive attributions:

  TEACHER: This work looks pretty good. Did you do well because you're really trying to use the writing strategy or because you were lucky to pick a topic that was easy to write about?

  JOHN: Well, the topic was easy, but I was trying to use the strategy.

- Teacher cues student to make positive attribution:

  TEACHER: This work looks pretty good. What did you do to get it to come out so well?

Students can also benefit from embracing productive beliefs about failure. They should be helped to understand that failure experiences are due in large part to persistence in using a less effective strategy and that efforts at using a more effective strategy are more likely to result in the level of success hoped for. The following example dialogue illustrates feedback being provided that incorporates this concept.

Example, As Applied to an Expository Writing Strategy

TEACHER: You don't look too happy about the results you got. Let's see if we can figure out the strategy you are using that's not working here. You seem to be using a writing strategy that doesn't include steps for thinking and organizing your thoughts before beginning to write. Although the strategy you've been using may work pretty well in some cases, it doesn't seem to be a good one to use for this type of assignment. What strategy do you need to try harder to use when defending a position?

8. *Effective feedback includes establishing goals for improving specific behaviors in subsequent attempts.* Many students with mild handicaps tend to depend on others for direction; they perform academic tasks because others (e.g., teachers) expect them to. Having students establish goals regarding future performance places more responsibility on them, tends to assure they understand the desired behavior, and plays an important motivational role (Adelman & Taylor, 1983; de Charms, 1976; Deshler, Schumaker, & Lenz, 1984; Ellis, 1986; Ellis, Lenz, & Sabornie, 1987b; Seabaugh & Schumaker, 1981). Thus effective feedback includes establishing goals for future performances that focus on improving specific types of behaviors. The following dialogue illustrates this practice.

PROBLEM

Jana is not effectively monitoring spelling errors when using an expository writing strategy.

Example Illustrating the Incorporation of Goal Setting into Feedback Routine

TEACHER: We've talked about the need to focus more on finding and correcting spelling errors in your writing. On the last essay you wrote about 60 words and misspelled 21 of them. Let's set a goal for reducing the number of spelling errors. How many spelling errors are you going to reduce it to?

STUDENT: Five errors.

TEACHER. That's a good goal, but it might be too big a jump from 21 errors. Let's set a goal that we think we can probably reach if we try to use the spelling strategy a little harder.

STUDENT: How about 10?

TEACHER: That would cut the number in half. Do you think you can write another 60-word essay but have only 10 spelling errors?

STUDENT: Yeah.

TEACHER: Okay. Getting it down to 10 is the goal. Once you've met that goal, maybe we can cut that one in half. Now, how are you going to work to accomplish your goal?

9. *Effective feedback is provided just before a practice attempt.* Most teachers believe that feedback is most effective when it immediately follows task performance. Although this is an important time to provide feedback, it is also important that students receive feedback immediately before beginning their next practice attempt. By reviewing feedback on previous performance and the goals established for the next attempt, the critical features of the correct behavior will be more likely to be incorporated into the student's upcoming practice attempt (Lenz, 1982).

10. *During the initial stages of practicing the strategy, feedback should be directive.* The teacher and student should identify the type of error made by the student and provide explicit feedback regarding the error.

Directive feedback is composed of two components. First, directive feedback focuses on examining the critical features that need to be performed correctly. Second, it involves modeling the correct procedure. When modeling, be sure to model the thought processes involved and point out the critical features of the overt behaviors. Subsequent modeling might involve having the student correct your performance. The following dialogue illustrates these ideas.

PROBLEM

When practicing an expository writing strategy, the student is not organizing thoughts before writing begins.

Directive Feedback	Features of Feedback
TEACHER: Remember that the prewriting phase of the strategy has four key	Establishing critical features of desired performance

parts. First, you need to establish an exact position. You're doing a good job there. Next, you need to think of two different reasons that tell why you have taken this position. Be sure to list both reasons before going any further. How many reasons do you list?

STUDENT: Two.

TEACHER: Right. Can they be similar, or should they be different?

STUDENT: Different.

TEACHER: Okay. After you have thought of two different reasons, you think about one of them and identify some things you can say that will explain the reason. You need to list at least three things to say about the reason.

Watch me do this part of the strategy. Listen to how I think as I am doing it.

I'm going to write about who I think is the best athlete. Let's see. There are a couple of athletes I think have been among the world's best whom I could write about. Bo Jackson is pretty good, but then so was Babe Ruth. Martina Navratilova is tops as well. But I have to make up my mind, one way or the other. Okay. I'm for Bo Jackson. He's the best. I need to make a note of it right here [writing on Organizer form].

Have I established an exact position? Yeah. I have. Now I need to think of two reasons why I think Bo is best. One is that he has played two different pro sports at once. So I list

Modeling use of critical features, thinking aloud

that reason here. Another is that he has won more awards than anybody. I write that here.

Now, before going any further, I need to make sure my reasons are different . . . two different sports at once . . . most awards . . . yeah, they're different enough. One is about playing different sports; the other is about winning a lot of awards.

Now I need to list some things to explain each reason. Let's see, what can I say about playing two sports? . . . football . . . baseball. I can also mention the teams . . . Raiders . . . Royals. I can also mention the positions he played in each sport . . . outfielder . . . running back. I need to make sure I listed at least three things to say about the first reason. Let me look . . . oh, yeah . . . I've listed a lot more than three. Now I need to think of what to say about the second reason . . .

After the teacher has modeled the desired behavior once, a second modeling may be necessary, only this time, the student could provide feedback as the teacher performs.

Directive Feedback

TEACHER: What will we do first?

STUDENT: Establish an exact position.

TEACHER: Then what do we check?

STUDENT: Make sure it's exact.

TEACHER: Then what will we do?

STUDENT: Think of a reason.

TEACHER: Then?

Features of Feedback

Establishing critical features of desired performance

STUDENT: Think of another reason.

TEACHER: What do we check now?

STUDENT: Make sure the reasons are different.

TEACHER: Then what do we do?

STUDENT: Think of things to say about the reason.

TEACHER: How many do we need, at least?

STUDENT: Three, at least three. More is better.

TEACHER: Let's do this prewriting part of the strategy together. This time I'll do it, but you tell me what to do. Let's see. The topic is "Should all teenagers try to go to college?" What do I need to do?

Student prompts teacher's behavior

STUDENT: Decide your exact position.

TEACHER: Okay. Let me think about that. College might not be necessary for some teenagers who plan on working in an area that doesn't require college, so my position is that I don't think that all teenagers should try to go to college. What do I do now?

STUDENT: List your first reason.

TEACHER: Do I need to check something about my position before listing the first reason?

STUDENT: Oh yeah. Make sure it's exact.

TEACHER: Okay. Let me check. It is. Now what do I do?

STUDENT: Think of a reason.

11. *When students are building fluency, feedback should be mediated.* Once students have mastered the basics of performing the strategy (e.g., your prompts are infrequently needed), the nature of feedback provided by you should shift from being directive (you diagnose the problem; you direct the desired behaviors) to being *mediative* (Ellis, Lenz, & Sabornie, 1987a; Stone & Wertsch, 1984; Vygotsky, 1978). Here, instead of diagnosing the problem yourself and directing students to perform the correct behavior, you merely cue students to diagnose the problem and to generate their own solutions. In mediated feedback, the responsibility for monitoring and adjusting behaviors shifts from the teacher to the student. Tables 4.1 and 4.2 contrast these two forms of feedback.

12. *When students have become fluent at using the strategy, feedback mediated by you should give way to being mediated only by the student.* Ultimately, students must take full responsibility for problem solving, including monitoring and analyzing their performance and structuring their own feedback. Students can easily become dependent on you to perform these processes for them or, at minimum, dependent on you to *cue* them to do so. Once students have established a fluent level of performance

TABLE 4.1. Directive Feedback (for Use When Students Are Unable To Perform Strategy Without Help)

STRATEGY	TYPE OF PROBLEM	WHAT TEACHER MIGHT SAY
Paraphrasing	Details selected and paraphrased are not relevant	"You need to think more about deciding which details to mention when paraphrasing the paragraph. They need to be relevant. That means important to remember. Listen to me think out loud as I read this next paragraph. Listen to how I think about the details . . ."
DEFENDS Writing Strategy	Off-topic sentence in middle of text	"You are clearly stating an exact position at the beginning of your essay, and then you start to explain your position by telling the first reason. You need to stick with the same position throughout the essay. Look at this sentence in the middle. It is too far off the topic of explaining how you feel about curfews. What do you need to do to fix this essay? . . ."

when performing the strategy, you should provide them with opportunities to practice using the strategy without receiving feedback from you or being prompted by you to give themselves feedback. When providing some of these practice opportunities, you can alert students prior to the activity that they should analyze their performance and provide themselves feedback. At other times, you should not cue them to provide themselves feedback either prior to or after performing the strategy. You should, however, monitor students' performance to assure it has not dropped off as a function of removing your cues. If you find that there is a consistent pattern of drops in performance as related to your removal of feedback prompts and cues, then you may wish to draw students' attention to the relationship between your cues, their performance, and what these behaviors mean to their ultimate independence.

TABLE 4.2. Mediative Feedback (for Use When Students Know How To Perform the Strategy but Are Practicing It To Build Fluency)

STRATEGY	TYPE OF PROBLEM	WHAT TEACHER MIGHT SAY
Paraphrasing	Main ideas and details paraphrased by student are not relevant	"Okay. Your paraphrase of the last paragraph was, 'The main idea of this paragraph is how to avoid blisters when hiking and two things to remember are to carry extra socks if needed and to wear bright clothes to prevent hunting accidents.' Is there a problem with the main idea or one of the details? . . . What do you need to do to fix it?"
DEFENDS Writing Strategy	Off-topic sentence in middle of text	"Show me what you think is best about your paragraph . . . Okay, check to see if you used the strategy to guide you all of the way through the essay . . . I see a problem; see if you can find it."

Selecting Materials for Practice

GOAL: To select materials for you and the student to use when practicing the strategy that are conducive to promoting the student's building confidence and competency.

ORIENTATION

Most strategies that a student will use for academic tasks will involve use of school materials (e.g., books, vocabulary lists, notes, quizzes). The materials a student is expected to use when first learning a strategy should not be highly challenging (e.g., require a high reading level). Remember, the student should have success when first using the strategy. The difficulty level (complexity) of materials and tasks that students attempt as they become proficient at the strategy should increase with continued practice using the new strategy. As mastery progresses, so should the difficulty level of the materials involved. This principle of selecting "considerate" materials (see Anderson & Armbruster, 1984) for strategy learning is no different from that used when selecting materials for any other task in the school day; first-grade readers are not typically expected to read Faulkner. In the SIM, the ideal difficulty level of materials to strive for is that necessary to use the strategy to meet normal demands of grade-appropriate work (typically in the regular classroom) and to use when adapting the strategy to meet demands of other settings.

FEATURES OF MATERIALS

Five features of materials should guide their selection for strategy learning and practice. These features include the materials' format, content, complexity, conducivity to strategy application, and applicability to other learning demands. Each is described below.

Format

The format of materials is the manner in which content and/or tasks are presented to students. For example, the information might be presented in an auditory format (e.g., paraphrasing information the teacher presents orally in class for the purpose of reducing note taking). Or the information might be presented in print format (e.g., if the students paraphrase a reading assignment). Of course, there is a great variety of ways to present information. In some instances information will be presented in multiple formats (e.g., the teacher orally provides additional content information as the student reads and paraphrases). Teaching students to use a new strategy such as The Paraphrasing Strategy will be easier if they first practice using the strategy on materials in a format that places few cognitive demands on them. Eventually, they should practice applying the strategy with more difficult and complex formats (e.g., paraphrasing the spoken and written information together).

Content

The content of materials is the information they present. For example, the content of a reading passage might be relatively familiar, entertaining, nonacademic or academic. Applying a strategy is generally easier when interacting with familiar or easily comprehended content. Once students have learned the basic procedures associated with using the strategy, they can learn to apply it to content that is less familiar or more difficult. This is the case regardless of how specifically the strategy is intended to enhance content comprehension (e.g., The Paraphrasing Strategy as compared to The FIRST-Letter Mnemonic Strategy).

Complexity

The complexity of materials does not refer to the intellectual challenge involved in understanding the content but rather to the way in which it is presented. (Of course, these two features can never be fully separated.) For example, the relative readability of written passages as traditionally estimated is thought to reflect the complexity of word identification and meaning comprehension. An equally important way to think of the passage's complexity is to consider how many sets of concepts are presented in the passage, how heavily comprehension of any one is dependent on comprehension of others, how succinctly they are conveyed, and how relevant the content is to the student's current knowledge. Learning how to apply a strategy such as Paraphrasing is easier when initially interacting with materials that are not highly complex (e.g., that clearly present content using words and sentence structures that are easily read).

Conducivity to Strategy Application

Materials should be selected based on their compatibility to strategy application. For example, it may be very easy to paraphrase the main idea of some paragraphs because of the way in which they are written (e.g., the main idea is virtually identified as such). In other paragraphs, however, the main idea may be very difficult to ascertain, therefore inhibiting the new strategy learner's success with the strategy. Conducivity to strategy application should be high during initial practice. At the point of virtual strategy mastery, less conducive materials are an appropriate challenge for the student.

Applicability to Other Demands

Because good strategy learners need to perceive the relevance of the strategies they are learning, the materials with which the strategies are learned should be useful for content-learning demands placed on the students. This will not always be easy given that students should learn the strategy using materials geared for success. For example, high school students with low reading levels who are studying chemistry for the first time may find that most easy-to-read science materials do not present the chemistry content they need to learn. In these cases the strategy should not be conceived of as competing with the chemistry content; each is important to learn. Materials related to other classes might better be used for initial strategy learning. In either case, the student should be guided to recognize the value of learning the strategy and in that way appreciate the content learned in the process, even when it cannot relate to other learning demands.

INCREASINGLY COMPLEX MATERIALS

Students learn a new strategy in order to be more successful at meeting a task demand. Eventually, students will practice applying the new strategy in the context of meeting such a demand. Students should first, however, learn how to perform basic processes and procedures associated with using the strategy. Initially, they should practice the strategy with materials in simple formats, the content of which is familiar to them and presented in a simple and straightforward manner. Performing the strategy when interacting with these materials should be relatively easy. Once students have learned to perform the basic processes and procedures associated with the strategy in relatively simple situations, they should practice applying it to the more difficult contexts that begin to approximate those found in grade-appropriate regular classroom work. For example, students might practice applying the DEFENDS Writing Strategy when responding to the mock social studies essay question, "Why did prohibition become a central issue of the 1920s?" Whenever possible, such tasks should be those of or related to the students' curricular demands.

The principle of controlling the difficulty of initial materials and the context in which the strategy is practiced is a well-documented instructional procedure. Numerous studies have shown that when these techniques are used, students with learning difficulties more readily learn the basic processes associated with performing the new strategy than when higher level materials are used (e.g., Ellis, Deshler, & Schumaker, 1989; Schmidt, 1983; Alley, Deshler, Clark, Schumaker, & Warner, 1983).

PART II

Teaching the Strategy

Pretesting and Obtaining a Commitment To Learn

GOAL: To identify the student's current abilities in relation to performing the strategy and establish the student's willingness to learn the strategy.

ORIENTATION

Learning strategies are taught with the intent of helping students learn in more efficient and effective manners than they already do. Short of standing over students with a gun, you cannot force them to be strategic against their will. Even if you did use a gun, sooner or later one of them might get the drop on you, and then where would you be? Much of schooling is not very different to students from being coerced at gunpoint. Students are often expected to perform tasks similar to those at which they have failed before. In addition, much of the content students learn and the means by which they learn it seem irrelevant to them. Thus, a good part of the students' day is spent doing tasks that are difficult and for which they will be corrected; in addition, the students are hard pressed to see the relevance of the tasks. These phenomena are not true because we believe that school should be taxing and unrewarding, but rather because learning is a challenging endeavor (and sometimes because we plan without thinking of the students' perspective). "Failures" along the way to success are common. For many students, however, success is rarely attained, and when it is attained, it too seems irrelevant. This scenario is particularly a problem for at-risk and low-achieving students for whom much of the school day is spent on unrewarding tasks or making small incremental gains.

Many students do have success at some points in the school day. Lots of students also have particular classes, teachers, and types of assignments that they like. Careful examination will almost always show that in these situations the students are motivated to learn. The topic, the teacher, or the activities are somehow interesting and fulfilling to the student. Motivated students are not always successful, but successful students are often motivated. Among the keys to motivation are to help students to recognize the need to learn (in this case to learn a new strategy) and to convince students that gains in learning will be made. When this is done in advance of learning, the student can express a commitment to learn.

PREPARATION

This stage of strategy instruction encompasses both pretesting and obtaining a commitment to learn. The pretest should be designed to (a) assess the student's current level of skills that are involved in performing the strategy and (b) reflect the type of tasks the student will be expected to do in regular class settings. In the case of some of the SIM strategies, pretests are included in the teacher's manual (e.g., FIRST-Letter Mnemonic) or suggestions for materials to use are provided (e.g., Paraphrasing). In other cases, you will need to devise your own pretest based on materials from the student's regular classes.

TIME CONSIDERATIONS

The amount of time required to complete the pretest will depend on the specific test being given and the performance skills of the student taking the test. The pretest should be scheduled at a time when the student can work unhurried and uninterrupted. Time should also be set aside to review the results of the pretest with the student. The sooner after completing the pretest the student receives feedback, the better. In this same meeting, the need to learn the new strategy should be established, and, after a general overview of the strategy, the student should be asked to make a commitment to learn it.

PROCEDURES

1. *Select an appropriate pretest.* Selecting an appropriate pretest may not be as easy as it sounds. The purpose is to test how well the student performs on a task calling for the strategy you hope to teach. If you are not careful, the pretest may not tap the same skills. For example, asking students to memorize a list of already familiar information or one that is very short is different from asking them to memorize a longer list of unfamiliar information. Be sure the pretest you select reflects both the skills addressed by the strategy and the types of tasks the student would actually be expected to complete using the strategy.

2. *Administer the pretest.* Begin by explaining to the students why you are giving this test. The students should understand that the purpose of a pretest is to determine what they can do in advance of learning the areas tested. This should serve to reduce test anxiety as well as to help the students work on the test earnestly. If they are "test-phobic," you do not need to call it a test. Although you may want to award students extra credit points for their pretest work, they should know in advance that their performance on this test will not affect their grade in any class.

Allow plenty of time for the test so that it can be completed uninterrupted. Whereas the "typical" situation in which the student may eventually perform the task may be full of disruptions and distractions, this situation should not be. The pretest is of what the student is currently *capable* of doing.

3. *Evaluate the pretest with students.* As soon as possible after the pretest is completed, evaluate it with the students. Ideally, this will be done as soon as they complete the pretest. Make certain that the students understand the scoring systems so that they may understand their own performance. Do not simply report a final score. Discuss what was done correctly and what was done incorrectly. Particularly when students have not done well, be sure to periodically remind them that this is a pretest. When possible have students help to evaluate their own work. For example, you may need to point out where an error was made, but once you

identify it, ask the student to explain why it is an error and how it might have been corrected.

4. *Discuss the value of learning the new strategy.* Unless the students have done quite well on the pretest, they probably need to learn the new strategy for the skills tested. Explain to the students, in fairly explicit detail, what the skill areas are in which they need improvement. Explain to the students that you know a learning strategy they could learn that would improve performance of this skill. (If the students are not already familiar with learning strategies, you will need to spend a few minutes discussing what they are and why they are valuable.) The SIM strategies teacher's manuals include information on the percentage of improvement students can expect to approximate if they learn and apply the strategy. These percentage improvement scores are derived from research studies used to validate the strategies before the manuals were published. Unless otherwise noted, the scores reflect the average performance of students with learning disabilities or at risk. In the case of the Paraphrasing Strategy, for example, students' performance on a comprehension pretest was 48%; average performance at posttest had improved to 84% (Schumaker, Denton, & Deshler, 1984). Such figures are very motivating to students, because they indicate that others like them who started out doing fairly poorly improved dramatically. If your students performed far more poorly than the average pretest score reported in the manual, be sure to point out that for that score to be an average, some of those students must have also started out with even lower scores.

5. *Obtain a commitment from students to learn the strategy.* The first step in obtaining a commitment from students to learn a new strategy is to help them articulate that success is possible. Review both how the strategy should help the student perform the skills necessary for success and the fact that success can be made in incremental gains if the student will persevere. Many students who are unmotivated are that way in part because it takes a long time to have success. Point out to students that you and they will be setting incremental goals that can be met reasonably. Students should understand that they will be able to see progress while in the process of learning.

Have students make a statement of commitment. This may be verbal or written. Some students like to have a contract. It need not specify any "dates of completion" (although general timelines are helpful), nor should it specify a "penalty" to be incurred if the student does not progress on schedule. The statement should identify the student, the strategy to be learned, and what the student will do to learn the strategy (in general). The statement should also mention the purpose or benefits of learning the strategy. There will be bad learning days, and reviewing the commitment at those times can bolster the student. If you know that an individual student gives up easily, include a statement indicating that she or he will persevere. The commitment can be included in the student's Individualized Education Program (IEP). It can also be posted in the classroom as an incentive. Students should be given their own copies. To authenticate the commitments, be sure both you and the students (and any other appropriate parties) sign it.

6. *Express a commitment to help the students learn the strategy.* Students should know that they will not be going it alone. You should express a commitment to helping them learn the strategy. This commitment can be stated in the same form as the students' commitment statement.

TROUBLESHOOTING

Sometimes the pretest backfires. You may give a pretest that was too easy for the student. The pretest performance may not reflect a strategy learning need when you know from observation that the student truly needs to learn a particular strategy. When this is the case, you should be honest with the student about whether another pretest more reflective of actual school tasks should be taken. Of course, you also need to be honest with yourself. Perhaps the student's pretest performance accurately indicates that she or he does not need to learn the strategy you have in mind. Reviewing the work samples and scenarios that led you to suspect the need in the first place can help you in sorting out the confusion.

There are students who will recognize their need to learn a strategy as well as the likelihood of the strategy helping them but who will still not commit to learning it. These students have truly low motivation. Other students just enjoy being obstinate (a conclusion we sometimes jump to too easily). In either case, you will probably desire to proceed with teaching the strategy. Do not be too quick to do so. Often, the students will not see things your way after a while. Students who are truly unmotivated to learn a strategy would only learn it half-heartedly at best. Work with the student to review the significance of the learning need. Also help the student to understand that many unsuccessful students have learned the strategy and have become successful by doing so. When possible, proceed with teaching the strategy to other students while the unmotivated one is near by. That student will be able to observe the others having success, which in itself may be convincing. If you simply cannot motivate a student to learn a particular strategy, do not force it. Perhaps the student needs to learn something else first, and one day you can return to the strategy. As frustrating as this may be, remember that one more unmotivating school experience can be far more frustrating for all involved.

Describing the Strategy

GOAL: To provide students with detailed descriptions of the strategy, how self-speech is used to regulate use of the strategy, and what will be involved in mastering the new strategy.

ORIENTATION

Much research has focused on identifying sets of best practices for teaching students to learn and use strategies. A number of instructional models have resulted. Among the most fruitful is Brown's (1978) Informed Training procedures. Students learn and use strategies more readily when they have been informed of the advantages of using them, as well as of when, where, and how to use them (e.g., Brown & Burton, 1978; Gagné & Brown, 1961; Roehler & Duffy, 1984).

Descriptions of strategy procedures and rationales for them should be conceived of separately to make certain each is adequately presented. In practice, however, these two types of information may overlap. For example, when describing the Paraphrasing Strategy, you may begin with the rationale for putting information in your own words. And, when describing procedures for putting the main idea and details into your own words, you may again provide a rationale for doing that. Although it is important to describe the overall, or fluid, process of a strategy, care should be taken to fully describe each step of the strategy individually.

When describing each strategy step, you should identify the critical overt and covert behaviors the step is designed to cue and explain why these behaviors are essential to the strategy's effectiveness (Ellis & Lenz, 1987; Roehler & Duffy, 1984). An example of an overt behavior during the Paraphrasing Strategy is to put the main idea in your own words. A covert behavior engaged during the strategy is reflecting on the content in the paragraph to determine what the main idea is. Appropriate performance of both overt and covert behaviors is critical to strategy effectiveness.

In addition to students having a basic understanding of steps the strategy is designed to have them do and how each is done, descriptions need to focus on how to use self-instruction to determine when to use the strategy, to help motivate oneself to perform the strategy, to cue the use of specific steps, and to monitor the effectiveness of the strategy (Ellis & Lenz, 1987; Meichenbaum, 1977; Roehler & Duffy, 1984; Wong, 1985). The effective strategy user "talks her/himself through" strategy performance. Finally, it is important that students be informed about what is involved in strategy mastery. Tell them about the various instructional stages involved in mastering the strategy and how long they can expect to spend working on learning it to mastery.

PREPARATION

A variety of materials are used to describe a strategy to students. These include materials the teacher and students will use only during demonstrations and some that students will continue to use as they begin to practice the strategy. Descriptions of materials essential to the SIM follow.

Strategy Notebooks or Folders for Students

During the course of learning a strategy, students may use many different materials (e.g., cue cards, progress charts). Organization of these materials can quickly become a problem if the students do not have a specifically designated place to store them. Students should have a three-ring notebook, so that items can be hole-punched, or a pocket folder.

Cue Cards Depicting the Strategy Steps

You will need to create a cue card (or several) that lists in order the steps of the strategy students will be learning. Cue cards should be prepared as transparencies for use on an overhead projector or as charts for the wall or copied onto a chalkboard. Also, students can be given copies of cue cards to keep in their notebooks. Alternatively, students can be prompted to take notes during strategy descriptions using the teacher's cue cards as models to create their own.

Figure 7.1 presents a sample cue card from the DEFENDS Writing Strategy. The cue card states each step exactly as students should learn it. It also highlights the mnemonic device used to remember the steps. Note in the figure that the steps of the strategy appear in large bold letters.

CUE CARD

DEFENDS

Decide on audience, goals, and position

Estimate main ideas and details

Figure best order of main ideas and details

Express the position in the opening

Note each main idea and supporting points

Drive home the message in the last sentence

Search for errors and correct

FIGURE 7.1. DEFENDS Steps Cue Card.

Cue Cards Depicting Key Information Related to the Rationale for Using the Strategy

Among the major goals of the "describe the strategy" instructional stage are to motivate students to learn the strategy and to provide them with information about where the strategy can be applied to help meet personal goals. Cue cards can be used as part of the advance organizer to identify specific settings for strategy use (e.g., school, work, and community) with a listing of examples for each setting.

Materials for Examples and Discussion

You may need some examples of the types of materials with which the strategy can be used as a reference when describing the application of the strategy. For example, a passage with several poorly organized paragraphs from a textbook might be used when teaching the DEFENDS Writing Strategy. A copy of a test from a social studies class might be used when describing a test-taking strategy.

Cue Cards Depicting Mastery Requirements

Effective strategy teachers clearly communicate performance expectations. This process can be facilitated by providing students with cue cards specifying these requirements. For example, you could create a cue card listing the types of errors you should not find once the SEARCH substrategy from DEFENDS has been used.

TIME CONSIDERATIONS

In most cases, a simple strategy can be fully described in 50 to 60 minutes of instruction. In cases where the strategy is more complex, the description may take two or three instructional periods. It is important to remember, however, that throughout all of the remaining stages of instruction this information will be repeatedly reviewed and discussed.

STRATEGY DESCRIPTION PROCEDURES

Providing a description of strategy procedures and rationale occurs in two phases, *orientation* and actual *description of the process:*

Phase I: Orientation

The purpose of the orientation phase is to provide an advance organizer for the description of the strategy. Advance organizers, which are used to prepare the student for what is to follow across each instructional stage of the SIM, are particularly important in this stage because the describe stage lays the foundation for the remaining stages of instruction. The orientation phase of the describe stage is very important as it includes information and instructional procedures that will be used throughout the instructional process.

1. *Define the Strategy.* One of the first pieces of information that students need in order to understand the purpose and processes of a strategy is a clear definition of the strategy and an explanation of the basic concepts that are included. A definition should include what the strategy will enable the student to do and the types of demands that the student will be able to meet by using the strategy. For example, an orientation description of the Paraphrasing Strategy might begin:

> Do you remember what a strategy is? Right. A strategy is a planful approach to a task. It includes how you think and act before, during, and after a task. It also includes how you evaluate the results of using the strategy. Today, we are going to begin to learn the Paraphrasing Strategy. Does anyone know what the word paraphrase means? No? It means to put an idea or something that you read into your own words. Can somebody tell us what I mean by that? [Solicit response.] Thank you; that was an example of a paraphrase. The Paraphrasing Strategy will help you learn how to approach reading tasks so that you can understand and remember more of what you read. This is a strategy that you may be able to use whenever you have to read something.

2. *Explain benefits.* Motivating students to want to learn that strategy is particularly important during the describe stage, because it is in effect part of an advance organizer for students practicing the strategy. One of

the best ways to motivate students to learn a new strategy is to provide them with information about what other students have experienced in learning the strategy. There are several ways of communicating these results. One is to provide students with before and after work samples of other students. For example, when teaching a Paragraph Writing Strategy, show students samples of paragraphs that were written by other students before instruction in the strategy and then following strategy instruction. Then ask students to compare the two. Also show students actual before and after data. For example, again show them that before learning the Paraphrasing Strategy, comprehension averaged 45%, whereas following mastery of the strategy, the comprehension of students averaged 85% (Schumaker et al., 1984). Another approach for sharing the results other students gained by using the strategy is having previous students speak with current students and share their experiences in learning the strategy.

Adolescents should be thought of as critical consumers. As a result, unless they understand the benefits, relative to their personal lives, of investing the time and energy required to master the strategy, their motivation will not likely be sustained throughout the learning process. Students need to be told why they should want to master the strategy and where in their personal world (school, employment, community, etc.) the strategy will be beneficial.

3. *Identify real assignments in specific classes where students could use the strategy.* As part of strategy performance, students must identify where, when, and under what circumstances the strategy can be used. Identify specific real-life situations in school for which using the strategy would be beneficial and discuss the characteristics of these situations. After identifying a few specific circumstances, ask students to provide additional ones. For example, specific real-life situations for using a Paragraph Writing Strategy include the weekly current-event reports that are required in Mr. Smith's social studies class and the lab reports that are required in Ms. Fibwot's biology class.

4. *Discuss stages of learning the strategy.* Up to this point, the focus of instruction has been on motivating students to learn the strategy by providing effective rationales for its use and discussing the results that can be expected. Unfortunately, many students often expect immediate results and do not realize that the strategy may be difficult to master and that practice and energy may be necessary. Therefore, inform students of what is involved in learning the strategy and approximately how much time and energy will be required of them. You should briefly describe each of the instructional stages and what the focus of the learning activities will be in each stage.

5. *Set goals for learning the strategy.* Goal setting is a motivational activity that should be employed throughout the instructional process. Students should be asked to establish two types of goals. The first is a goal related to the student's performance in a setting in which she or he is currently participating. A variety of goal statements can be constructed by students. The following statements provide examples of the types of goal statements that might be prompted.

- I want to improve my work in Mr. Jones's social studies class.

- One of the things I can do is to write better current-event reports.

- Using the DEFENDS strategy will help me reach this goal.

The second type of goal to be prompted focuses on completing specific stages in the learning process. Using a calendar, you should help students establish specific dates by which they hope to complete each stage in learning the strategy. Later, the students should monitor their progress toward meeting these timelines and adjust their goals accordingly.

6. *Make an instructional decision: Are students ready for the next phase of instruction?* The teacher must determine whether students are ready to learn the new strategy at this point. Students are ready to learn the specific aspects of the new strategy if they:

- can describe the rationale for learning the new strategy in their own words,

- can identify at least two specific settings in which using the strategy would be beneficial, and

- have established goals for learning the strategy.

If students have not accomplished these instructional objectives, additional instructional time may need to be spent. It is not likely that the student will become invested in the learning process if these objectives have not been addressed.

Frequently, students may not appear to be motivated to learn the strategy. The lack of apparent motivation is a common and persistent problem among adolescents with a history of low achievement and/or learning disabilities (LD). Identifying the problem is particularly difficult because many adolescents may be sufficiently motivated to learn the strategy but choose to hide their motivation for several reasons, including not wishing to appear to their peers as academically invested and not wanting the teacher to establish high expectations for them. Other students may simply not want to apply their energy to a task they do not value. Their personal beliefs about the value of academic tasks and learning may be negative and well ingrained. Some students may have developed the belief that they are "dumb" and nothing is going to help; others may believe that failure is inevitable, thus seeing no reason to set themselves up for yet another opportunity to fail; some students may believe that the strategies they are currently using are effective and resist learning a new strategy.

Continue to teach the strategy to those students who appear to be relatively unmotivated to learn the procedure. Often, once students experience some success, the enabling power of the new strategy will provide sufficient intrinsic motivation for students to continue. Do not, however, attempt to teach the strategy to those students who are *strongly* resistant to learning it. Proceed with instruction with the remaining students, but allow the reluctant student to witness the success classmates are experiencing with the new strategy. This student may eventually wish to be included. When resistance is high enough, the student will refuse to learn the new strategy, and valuable teaching and learning time will have been wasted.

Phase II: Description of the Process

The purpose of this phase is to describe in detail each step of the strategy. You should describe what the step cues the student to do, how to perform the overt actions associated with each step, what the strategy user should think about as part of performing each step (the covert actions), and why the individual steps are critical to the overall problem-solving process. Six specific teaching steps are involved in describing the strategy process.

1. *Preview the steps of the strategy.* Description of the strategy should begin by informing the students as to how many steps are involved in the strategy and cueing them to take notes as each is presented. Some teachers prefer to give students a cue card or sheet of paper with the strategy

steps listed on it, believing that students should focus all of their attention on the description. Other teachers have argued that the requirement of note taking prompts a more typical secondary school response and promotes more active cognitive engagement. Both positions are reasonably correct; teachers should select the most appropriate methods based on the skills and needs of their students.

2. *Describe each step.* Begin by describing what the student must do, that is, the procedural element of the step that must be accomplished if the step is to be performed correctly. For example:

> *The first step of the FIRST-Letter Mnemonic Strategy involves looking at the first letter in each of the items of your list to see if the first letters can form a word.*

The name of the step should be written on the board or emphasized to focus the students' attention on the key action involved in the step. Second, the teacher should elaborate on the procedures for this step by explaining what the student should think about during the step and pointing out important overt behaviors in performing it. For example:

> *Begin by looking at the list exactly as it is presented. A word that you know may jump out at you. Or you might make up a nonsense word that you could remember. However, you need to ask yourself if there is a word or a nonsense word formed by the first letters that could help you remember this important list. If you don't see a word or if you don't think you can remember a word that you have formed, you can go to the next step . . .*

As demonstrated, an important consideration is thinking about how to decide when to go on to the next step of the strategy. Before moving on to the next step of the strategy, however, the teacher should provide a brief model of how that step is performed. This model should not be extensive. It should be brief and to the point. It should appear easy and successful. For example:

> *I have a list here of the five characteristics of the definition of a colonization:*

> **Characteristics of Colonization**
>
> group of people
>
> ruled by a mother country

> organized for common good
>
> underdeveloped area
>
> plans for permanent settlement

This is a list that will probably be on the test, so I want to try to remember it. Let me see if I can take the first letter of each of my listed items and form a word out of them. I will write each of the letters out horizontally—G R O U P—Hey, this is great! I see the word GROUP. I have formed a word. And the word GROUP relates to colonization. This is going to really help me to remember this list.

Each strategy step will cue students to perform covert cognitive processes. Give particular attention to identifying these cognitive processes and determining how to describe them overtly, or at least try to identify mechanisms that will help students organize and guide their thoughts in performing the processes involved. For example, a step of the Paraphrasing Strategy cues the reader to apply specific cognitive processes associated with identifying main ideas. There might be a variety of cognitive processes involved in generating a main idea, but one you might describe to students is "Read a little, say to yourself what this seems to be about, and then read some more to see if that is what it is about." Finally, the student is asked to paraphrase at least one main idea and two details in the paragraph. The teacher can help the student think about this by prompting the student to organize thoughts using sentence starters such as "This paragraph is about _____."

3. *Present the remembering system.* The focus of presenting the strategy thus far has been on helping students to understand the overt and covert performance of each step. After the strategy has been presented, the focus of instruction should turn to identifying a remembering system. The teacher does this in two ways. First, point out the mnemonic device remembering system that has already been created for the strategy. For example, for the DEFENDS Writing Strategy, point out that the first letters of each step spell the word DEFENDS. Second, try to connect the remembering system to the processes involved in the strategy or to the tasks associated with the strategy. In the case of DEFENDS, you might point out how the word *defend* relates to backing up a position or an idea.

4. *Compare the new strategy to students' old habits.* One of your goals is for students to clearly understand how the new strategy differs from those strategies (or nonstrategic practices) that have been used in the past to meet task demands. After presenting the strategy steps to the students, ask them to comment on how the new strategy is similar to or different from how they have approached similar tasks in the past.

5. *Provide a post organizer.* Review the steps of the strategy and its uses. For this review try not to belabor any one step; help the students to think about the complete strategy as a fluid process. Check to see if students understand the strategy and see the relationship between its use and meeting the demands of settings. If students appear to understand the strategy and its relevance, then move on to the next phase of the SIM instructional process.

6. *Make an instructional decision: Are students ready for the next phase of instruction?* Students are ready to proceed to the modeling stage of instruction when they are able to:

- describe specifically what each step in the strategy is cueing them to do, and

- tell how the new strategy is similar to or different from strategies they have used in the past to complete similar tasks.

Modeling the Strategy

GOAL: To model how to use a strategy to appropriately complete a task, so that the student can understand the key processes involved.

ORIENTATION

Modeling is probably the most important stage in the SIM teaching process. The purpose of modeling is to promote student understanding of how to perform the strategy being learned. Effective modeling includes demonstration of both the physical behaviors and the cognitive processes involved in strategy performance. Modeling is an early stage in the instructional process so that students will have knowledge of how to correctly perform the strategy as they learn it. Modeling is also a tool that can be used anywhere in the instructional process. Modeling can be incorporated into describing a strategy, or it can be used as part of providing feedback on performance or as the focus of an entire instructional lesson. It may be used whenever students need insight into a process in which they are to engage.

Many of the procedures involved in modeling SIM strategies are based on procedures described by Finch and Spirito (1980) and Meichenbaum (1977). These researchers have demonstrated that individuals' verbalization of what they are doing helps guide correct learning of a procedure.

Meichenbaum described a set of steps associated with leading the student to this verbalization process. First, the teacher performs the task while speaking aloud what he or she is thinking. As instruction proceeds the student is prompted to perform the task and think out loud under the teacher's guidance. Gradually the teacher's prompts are faded out and the student fades the thinking out loud to a whisper and finally to private speech that takes place "in the head." Many of us followed a similar process when as children we learned to tie our shoes: "Take a lace in each hand, cross one over and under, pull tight, make a loop . . ." Every once in a while as adults, we tangle our laces and carefully review our process using the same steps we once vocalized. This is the goal of thinking aloud during modeling—to provide students with a model of speech they can use from the beginning of learning a strategy right through applying it as experts.

PREPARATION

Modeling episodes can be prepared in advance of a lesson or be spontaneous when their use is evident. Careful preparation is definitely required, however, before engaging in the initial modeling stage of strategy instruction. This modeling must reflect expert strategy usage. Begin preparation by identifying typical content and situations with which the strategy will be taught. These content and situations will logically be representative of those to which the student will be expected to apply the strategy. Practice modeling the strategy to yourself. Plan when and how you will model each part of the strategy during instruction and how you will model thinking aloud. The first few times you practice, the think-aloud aspect of modeling may be a source of personal revelations about your own strategy process. Be sure to earnestly practice thinking aloud; the students do not need to be confused as you work through your own clarifications on how to perform the strategy. Initial modeling needs to demonstrate how to correctly perform the strategy. You would, however, be wise to build in some preplanned problems so that students can observe how you monitor and problem solve. Make sure that you select a task that you can complete and that you provide a full model of all the steps of the strategy.

Physically, the model must be performed so that all students can see and hear all of the phases of the modeling process. For small groups the model may be conducted at a table. An overhead projector with transparencies of the text or materials that will be used in the modeling is better with larger groups.

TIME CONSIDERATIONS

If you try to verbalize every thought you have about implementing a strategy, you are going to make the strategy appear overly complex, and the model will take too long to complete. The model should provide quick but accurate insights into how to think about the task of performing the strategy. The first models that you present are probably going to include more verbalizations on what to do than on how to think. Until the students understand the physical elements, it is reasonable to not focus too much on the thinking-aloud aspects of the model. However, as strategy instruction proceeds, instruction in the cognitive elements should be emphasized. This is particularly true for complex strategy systems involved in such tasks as taking notes, reading a textbook, studying, and taking a test. Such strategy systems rely heavily on thinking through their processes.

INSTRUCTIONAL PROCEDURES

There are four stages to the modeling process, whether it is being done for the modeling stage, as part of feedback, or for some other purpose. First, an advance organizer is provided for the modeling episode. Second, the teacher performs the physical or cognitive model. Third, students are enlisted in the modeling process. Fourth, a post organizer is provided covering what has been learned in the modeling episode.

Phase I: Advance Organizer for the Modeling Process

Use an advance organizer to introduce your students to the modeling, whether or not they are already familiar with modeling. Following the advance-organizer guidelines presented in Chapter 3, you will ensure that students:

- know that you are going to provide a model and that they will be enlisted in the modeling process after they have had a chance to observe you,

- understand what a model is and can identify situations where they have observed models,

- can describe how modeling will help them understand and perform the strategy,

- have an opportunity to preview what will be modeled so that they can be informed as they observe implementation of the strategy, and

- understand that they are expected to ask questions as they observe in preparation for their own participation in the modeling process.

Phase II: Present the Model of the Strategy

1. *Model the approach to the task while thinking aloud.* As you begin your model, describe the context for it. For example:

> *Okay, I am sitting in science class and the teacher, Ms. Pierce, has just handed back my homework from the night before. I look at the answers to my questions and see that I have missed three or four. My assignment now is to go back to the science book to find the correct answers. So I reach for my science book and I look at the table of contents to see what page Chapter 4 starts on . . .*

If there are signals or conditions that have been identified that indicate when to use a specific strategy, you should model how these are identified. For example, if the guideline that has been presented is "Use this strategy whenever you come to an illustration in a text," you should model encountering an illustration while reading and talk about how strategy use should begin.

2. *Model self-instruction while thinking aloud.* As soon as you have modeled the selection of a strategy, modeling of the self-instruction process should begin. You begin this by asking yourself about the mnemonic device for recalling the strategy, vocalizing the steps of the strategy, or writing the strategy on scratch paper as a reminder of the steps. Here are a couple of examples:

Okay, I want to use my Summarizing Strategy. Let's see, the word to remind me of the steps is . . . The first step is . . . In that step I want to . . . Okay, let me try it . . . To start the first step, I . . .

So I don't forget, I am going to write the mnemonic device for this strategy on the corner of my paper. I will want to erase it when I am done, so I want to make sure I write lightly and very small . . .

As you complete each strategy step, you return to the self-instructional process. You ask yourself what the next step is and review it briefly before you begin it. This process is repeated for each step until the task is completed.

3. *Model self-monitoring while thinking aloud.* As each step is completed, begin to model the self-monitoring process. Self-monitoring involves asking yourself questions about how the strategy is working and the correctness or accuracy of responses, and checking your progress toward task completion.

Let me check to see if that is right . . . Hmm, when I began I forgot to . . . I better do this over . . . Good, that's correct . . . It seems to make more sense now.

4. *Model problem solving while thinking aloud.* During the process of self-monitoring, problem solving should be included. That is, as you model the process of checking your progress or work and something is wrong, model asking yourself the question *What should I do?* This will lead you into opportunities to model the problem-solving process. When you model problem solving, you should show the process of identifying the alternatives that you can think of, exploring the alternatives as they might relate to best and worst outcomes, selecting alternatives that you judge to most likely result in success, trying the selected alternative, reflecting on its success (i.e., is it both effective and efficient?), and determining if you can continue or if the problem still exists. If the problem still exists, you should model how you return and go through the problem-solving process again.

Hmm . . . this doesn't work . . . Let's see what I can do . . . If I _____, then _____ will happen. If I _____, then it might cause _____. How about _____? Hmmm . . . Yes, I think I will try _____, because . . . This seems to work. Now, I can continue.

It is a good idea to plan these problems as a part of the model so that you can anticipate confusion and provide a clear picture of the problem-solving process. Try to recall some of your own confusion as you first learned the strategy. The model will be most useful if it is relevant to problems your students will actually have.

5. *Model how the task is performed while thinking aloud.* As you demonstrate the strategy, actually perform the task. Be sure that you do not overemphasize the cognitive aspects of the strategy and neglect the physical aspects of the strategy. You should show students what to do and describe it as you are doing it. Don't just say, "Now I would do this . . . then I would do this . . ."

> Now I am turning the page. I am going to write the title of the chapter in my notes over on this part of the paper [point]. Can everyone see where I am putting the title? Good. Okay, now I have written the title down. Now I need to ask myself . . .

6. *Model self-evaluation and self-reinforcement while thinking aloud.* As tasks are completed and eventually the entire strategy is completed, you should model how you evaluate your overall performance on the task and the overall strategy.

> Did I complete the task the way I was supposed to? Did I do the strategy correctly? Does what I did make sense to me?

In addition to the self-evaluation, you should model affirmations related to your successes. You want to show students how to encourage their own progress and how to take a positive approach to making mistakes.

> Boy, I am doing really great! This is easy! This strategy really helps me to organize!

The process of self-reinforcement should continue throughout all phases of the model, including when the strategy is completed as well as when the modeling episode is concluded.

Phase III: Enlist Student Assistance in the Model

Once you have briefly modeled the entire strategy, begin to enlist the help of students in the strategy model. Students should use their notes or cue cards for the strategy as they help model how the strategy is applied. The teacher should prompt the students to "talk through" what must be done to perform the strategy and to help talk through decisions related to completing each step. To accomplish this, the teacher should select a task that is easy for all the students in the group to perform. Students should be reminded to look at their notes to help them remember what to do and to ensure that they monitor that the strategy is being performed correctly.

1. *Prompt student involvement.* Once you, the teacher, have provided a model of the strategy from beginning to end, invite the students to participate in a second modeling. Enlist the students' help by prompting them to name "the next step." You may ask, "What do I do in this step?" As a rule of thumb, students should be prompted to respond and become involved in the model at the rate of approximately one student statement per every three statements made by the teacher. Following this rule will help to ensure that students begin to assume responsibility for verbalizing strategy procedures. As the shared modeling phase continues, the students' statements should become longer and the teacher's statements should become shorter.

> *Okay, I've got you started, now what's next? What's the next step? How do we do that step? What questions should you be asking yourself?*

2. *Prompt students to think aloud.* In the early stages of strategy learning, students may have some difficulty with the think-aloud part of strategy performance. Their verbalizations may be very procedural. Thinking aloud is not common to students. The teacher should continue to model these processes, reinforcing students who correctly model them and prompting students to try to express their thoughts.

> *What would you say to yourself as you complete that step? Tell us what you are thinking. What should you be asking yourself at this point? Okay, remember to think out loud. Describe what you are doing and thinking. Now, what would you say to yourself?*

3. *Check student understanding.* A major purpose of the student enlistment in the modeling stage is to check to see if students understand what the strategy is all about and if each step is clearly understood. Therefore,

the teacher's prompts should encourage responses that will allow the teacher to check understanding of the strategy and its application.

Explain what you are supposed to do here. Why did you do that? Show us what you do here and explain it as you do it. What is involved in that step?

4. *Shape, expand, and correct student responses.* The student enlistment phase enables the teacher to teach the student, immediately correcting misunderstandings. As students become involved the teacher should prompt them to elaborate on their comment and guide them to monitor performance, self-correcting incorrect responses. This is accomplished by asking questions that lead students to the correct response, asking students to explain their answers, informing students when they have misinterpreted the process or have fallen back on old habits that have not been successful, and, of course, praising good efforts.

That was good; now what do you need to do? . . . Right! During this step you need to say to yourself . . . Can you explain to me what you understand? Good, now do it . . . Right, but don't forget to . . . Let's try it again . . . Okay, stop; in this part we need to . . . What did you do? . . . Let's try it again This time remember to . . . Great job! Why did that work?

5. *Engineer student success.* Finally, it is important that as students become involved they experience success. Therefore, the good teacher mediates the learning process so that the students understand how to correctly perform the strategy, in fact correctly perform the strategy, and know that they have done so.

You are doing fine. Now do this . . . Okay, do it again , try this . . . Good. Wait a minute, what does the cue card say? That's right; now go ahead . . . Great, you did it! See, this is going t be easy for you. Let's do it again, but this time let's take it slower. I think you will find it easier if you use your cue cards a little more.

Phase IV: Provide a Post Organizer

Using the post organizer framework presented in Chapter 3, bring the modeling lesson to closure. As part of the post organizer, ensure that students:

- understand the strategy,

- understand that they should continue to think aloud when they perform the strategy in the future, and

- know what they will be doing next in the sequence of strategy instruction.

Prompting Verbal Elaboration and Rehearsal of the Strategy

9

> **GOAL:** To facilitate students' comprehension and retention of strategy procedures via their use of appropriate language to mediate strategy applications.

ORIENTATION

To be effective strategy users, students need to fully understand what they are doing and why they are doing it. Facilitating student verbal elaboration of a strategy (describing and explaining the strategy in their own words) can be an effective technique for promoting comprehension of what is being learned.

Effective use of a strategy involves self-regulation of the critical processes used when performing it. Having students verbally elaborate on the critical processes can promote their more effective self-regulation (Deshler, Warner, Schumaker, & Alley, 1983). We often talk to ourselves, or use self-speech, to help analyze a situation, plan what to do, execute the plan, and monitor its effectiveness (Bruer, 1993; Vygotsky, 1978). When learners translate to-be-learned information into their own wording, they are more likely to associate the new information with existing knowledge.

Students' comprehension and recall of information is improved when their elaborations are precise (e.g., Bransford & Stein, 1984; Wong & Sawatsky, 1984). Successful learners tend to make precise elaborations, whereas students who have not been successful learners tend to make less accurate and complete elaborations Thus, when describing in their own words what a strategy is designed to do, why it works, and when it might be used, less successful students are more likely to omit essential information and fail to fully comprehend the new strategy. Brown (1978) noted that when students do not understand the various dimensions of a strategy, it is not likely to be used in real-life situations. When facilitating use of verbal elaboration, you will need to monitor what students say and provide feedback to ensure precise elaborations.

Because the steps of the strategy are essentially the "plan to follow," it is important to remember the steps. Therefore, an essential component of effective strategy instruction is having students memorize the steps of the strategy. Once they have done so, the students can use self-speech to independently instruct themselves in what to do when applying the strategy. How to use verbal elaboration as an instructional technique is described in this section.

PREPARATION

Preparation to do verbal elaboration is minimal. You probably prepared all of the materials that you will need (e.g., student cue cards or notes, overhead transparencies of the strategy steps) when you were preparing to describe and model the strategy.

TIME CONSIDERATIONS

When students are initially learning a new strategy, verbal elaboration activities to enhance comprehension of the strategy may last as long as 20 to 30 minutes. Later, as students are learning how to apply the strategy, advance organizers should include opportunities for review via verbal elaboration. All of the advance organizer activities should be completed in less than 5 minutes.

INSTRUCTIONAL PROCEDURES

In SIM strategies instruction, there are three phases to the verbal elaboration and rehearsal part of instruction: orientation, verbal elaboration, and verbal rehearsal.

Phase I: Orientation

Provide an advance organizer. If the focus of the lesson is on facilitating verbal elaboration of the strategy, tell the students that they will be learning to describe the strategy using their own words. In addition, they will be learning to associate the key action steps represented in the mnemonic remembering system with implementation of the strategy. The focus during the verbal rehearsal phase will be on memorizing the remembering system and the key action steps of the strategy to a fluent level so that practice in applying the strategy to specific tasks can then begin.

Phase II: Verbal Elaboration

1. *Facilitate student elaboration of the overall strategic process.* The initial focus of this instruction is on facilitating students' elaboration of what the strategic process is designed to accomplish (i.e., not on the names or processes of the specific steps of the strategy) and what the general process involves. Students should also be able to describe the purpose of the strategy. The first time you do this activity with your students, it may be desirable to model the elaboration.

> *What I want you to do is tell me in your own words what this strategy is all about. If I were describing it in my own words, I might say, "The Paraphrasing Strategy is about reading short sections and then stopping and summarizing each section using my own words. Putting it into my own words ensures I really understand it. Summarizing small sections as I read will help me remember what I read." Now, if someone asked you to tell them what the Paraphrasing Strategy is for, what would you say?*

Because the emphasis is on facilitating comprehension of the strategy, rather than on memorization of the strategy, students should be allowed to look at their notes and cue cards of the strategy steps as needed. This activity should continue until the students are able to describe the overall process involved in using the strategy, as well as the reasons for using it.

2. *Facilitate student elaboration of each step of the strategy.* As soon as students are able to describe and explain the overall process of applying the strategy, the focus of instruction should shift to facilitating their elaboration of the specific strategy steps. Here students, while looking at a list of the strategy steps, describe what each step is designed to do and why it is an important component of the overall strategic process.

> *Look at the first step of the strategy. Tell me in your own words what this step is cueing you to do. Why is it important to do this step?*

3. *Facilitate student elaboration on the role of self-instruction.* Earlier, when you were describing the nature of the strategy and how the strategy would be learned, you introduced the concept of self-instruction to students. Now you want to ensure that students understand the role of self-instruction in effective use of the strategy. Thus, your goal is to enable students to describe, in their own words, how self-instruction is used to regulate performance of the strategy steps. Because self-instruction may be a novel concept for many students, you may need to model how to elaborate on the purpose of using self-instruction.

> *Next, I want you to tell me, using your own words, why you need to talk to yourself when using the strategy. What are some of the things you might say to yourself?*
>
> *If I were asked to do this, I might say, "When using the Paraphrasing Strategy, I need to follow the strategy steps so I can reach my goal of remembering more of what I read. I'll be telling myself what to do next as I'm using the strategy. If I can't remember what to do, I'll think of the letters in the remembering device to help me think of the next step.*
>
> *"I might also be talking to myself as I read. For example, if I read the sentence 'There are many reasons why people like to vote,' I might say to myself, 'I need to remember the important details from this paragraph—this sounds like some important details will follow; I'll try to spot them."*
>
> *"I might also be talking to myself to motivate myself and build confidence. I might say things to myself like 'I'm getting good at this,' or 'This works pretty well.'*
>
> *"I might also say things to myself to monitor how it's going as I perform the strategy. I might say things like, 'Let's see, how do I know that is actually the main idea? Should I change it?' "*

4. *Promote verbal elaboration in large groups.* Having each individual student provide verbal elaborations directly to you is not always feasible when working with a large class. You may wish to consider incorporating grouping or even cooperative learning techniques. You should keep in mind, however, that the students' accurate feedback to each other is critical to this process. Regardless of the activity you design to facilitate verbal elaboration, make sure that there is a system for providing feedback to students and that each student has an opportunity to make precise elaborations.

An activity you may wish to use involves pairing students. Each student provides an elaboration and is checked by a partner. Or small groups (3 to 5 students) can work together to develop a "telegram" describing the strategy. Groups are then asked to share their elaborations with the other groups. To ensure that individual students can elaborate the strategy, each individual might be required to describe the new strategy on a subsequent test question. You can also have small groups of students compose a news item for the school paper describing the strategy and why, when, and where it might be used. An effective activity for a large group involves having students form two concentric circles. Each student on the outside circle is paired with a corresponding student on the inside circle. Then the teacher asks students on the outside circle to tell their partners about a specific aspect of the strategy (e.g., "Describe to your partner what the last step of the Paraphrasing Strategy is cueing you to do"). The inner-circle partner then checks the student's precision of the elaboration. Next, the teacher asks students on the inner circle to rotate their circle two places, creating new pairs of students. Inner-circle students are then asked to make an elaboration, as outer-circle partners check for precision. This process is repeated until all aspects of the strategy have been elaborated upon. Since each pair of students is speaking simultaneously, the procedure is noisy, but fun and effective.

5. *Make an instructional decision.* Most students will be able to verbally elaborate on the strategy if you have effectively described and modeled it beforehand. On occasion, however, you will encounter a student who does not appear to have the verbal skills requisite to these activities, and you may be tempted to consider not requiring this student to make elaborations. Before deciding to exempt the student from making verbal elaborations, consider the following:

- The student's inability to describe the overall strategic process, the steps of the strategy, and/or how self-instruction is used may be due to insufficient describing and modeling on your part rather than on the lack of verbal skills on the student's part. You may want to provide additional instruction in these areas and prompt elaboration a second time.

- Excusing students from making verbal elaborations reduces the opportunity to learn how to use very powerful learning techniques associated with self-regulation. If students cannot make verbal elaborations, teaching them how to perform these critical learning processes is better than allowing them to continue to be ineffective.

- Memorization of the strategy steps is likely to proceed much faster if sufficient time and energy are allotted to elaboration of the strategy steps first.

If students are experiencing difficulty performing verbal elaborations, try using chaining techniques. Here, you say the first part of the elaboration and have the student finish the sentence.

> *The first step of the DEFENDS Writing Strategy is "Decide on audience, goals, and position." That means that I need to think about . . . (cue student to finish the sentence).*

Another technique to facilitate elaboration is to write on the board or a piece of paper key words or phrases that can be used to cue the student what to say.

> What is the strategy?
>
> What should happen if I use the strategy?
>
> When should I use the strategy?
>
> Where can I use the strategy?

Then you point to or read each key phrase and ask the student to respond.

Phase III: Verbal Rehearsal

1. *Facilitate student memorization of the strategy steps.* Once students are able to describe the overall strategic process as well as each step in the process, they are well on their way toward comprehending the strategy. The next step in this stage of instruction is to have them commit the strategy steps to memory. In this phase, the steps of the strategy are memorized to a fluent 100% mastery level, so naming steps can readily serve as self-instructional cues for what to do as the strategy is performed. As students move to this phase of instruction, inform them of the shift and the criteria for mastery.

If the strategy you are teaching has been encapsulated using a remembering device, (e.g., the first letters of each step in the DEFENDS Writing Strategy spells the word DEFENDS), be sure the student recognizes the mnemonic characteristics of the words (DEFENDS, as in defending a point of view) and can spell it. Then show the student how the first letters can be used to help recall the strategy step.

2. *Model and conduct a group rehearsal.* The first step in prompting students to begin the process of committing to memory the remembering system of the strategy is to teach them what it is that they are expected to do. Therefore, it is important for you to begin this process for modeling the rehearsal process at the mastery level that is expected (i.e., 100% accuracy). The model should include the:

- Name of the strategy (e.g., "This is the DEFENDS Writing Strategy"),

- Name of the remembering system (e.g., "I remember it by the word DEFENDS"),

- Remembering cue for each step (e.g., "The *D* signals the first step, . . ."), and

- Recall of each step and substep (e.g., "Decide on audience, goals, and position . . .")

After modeling, the teacher informs the group that each member of the class will be expected to individually demonstrate mastery of the remembering system for the strategy. While allowing students to glance at their cue cards, notes, or a list of the steps somewhere in the classroom, ask students, one at a time, to name one part of the remembering system.

What is the strategy we are learning, Julia? Good! What is the remembering system that we use for this strategy, Jose? Yes! What is the first step of the strategy, Dan? That's right, we decide our position, but what is the whole step? Right, we Decide on audience, goals, and position. What's next, Dee? . . .

As students learn the process of group rehearsal, the teacher can begin to drop the verbal prompts and statements and can simply point to students for the next step. If a student falters the teacher can assist the student. The goal is to make the students feel comfortable with the group rehearsal process and to teach them how group rehearsal is conducted.

3. *Prompt peer-assisted and individual rehearsal.* Once the students learn the group rehearsal process and the expectations for this type of practice are established, the teacher can allow students to work individually or in peer-assisted instructional arrangements to rehearse and memorize the remembering system for the strategy. Although individual students must ultimately be responsible for memorizing the strategy steps, there are a number of peer activities that can be used to facilitate this goal. One technique is to place students into small groups of 3 to 5 students. Group members are responsible for studying together, drilling each other, and so forth. Groups compete with each other to be the first to have all members memorize the strategy steps. One way to evaluate individual mastery of the steps is through public recitation of the steps of the strategy. Volunteers from each group can stand up and attempt to recite the strategy steps. Members of the other groups monitor the students and call them "safe" if all the steps are named correctly and fluently or "out" if the students falter or make a mistake. Then another member from a different group has a turn. The procedure continues until each group member is declared "safe." Procedures such as this one are best used with students who are not highly competitive or degrading to each other.

4. *Conduct a rapid-fire verbal rehearsal.* After sufficient opportunity has been given for students to memorize the remembering system, it is important to emphasize speed and fluency in the recall of the steps. This can build students' confidence in their ability to remember the strategy. Rapid-fire rehearsal is a technique that can be used to facilitate the development of fluency. This is done by having students sit so that each student can see the teacher easily and the teacher can see each student. This can often be accomplished by having students form a semicircle with their desks. The teacher then points to students in a random fashion and has them name the next strategy step. At the beginning of this activity, strategy steps are visible to students (written on the board, on a handout, etc.) and they are allowed to look at them if needed. Later, the steps should be removed from view so that students are required to recall them from memory. Gradually the pace of the rehearsal process is increased. The rapid-fire rehearsal process is conducted until the students are able to state each of the steps of the strategy fluently and accurately.

Regardless of the method used to facilitate memorization of the strategy steps, students should be individually quizzed to determine whether they can name them fluently and accurately; 100% mastery should be required. These quizzes can take the form of individual oral quizzes or traditional written tests in which students write the steps of the strategy from memory.

5. *Make an instructional decision.* A common perception of many students with learning disabilities and other low-achieving students is that they do not possess the abilities to memorize the steps of a new strategy. You may have some of these students and be tempted to not require them to memorize the strategy steps. Before making this decision, consider the following:

- Many students possess the ability to memorize information, but they often do not know how to memorize. In such cases, you need to teach these students how to use verbal rehearsal and self-checking to memorize the strategy steps.

- Many students may be attempting to avoid difficult tasks by feigning disabilities (e.g., lack of memorization abilities). Some students with a history of failure will attempt to manipulate situations so that they are not required to perform some tasks. The expectation for students to memorize the information may need to be reinforced and maintained.

- If students do not commit the strategy to memory, it is likely that learning to apply the strategy will require considerably more time, energy, and practice. An increased number of failure experiences will also occur because students will not be able to use self-instruction effectively. As a result, the decision to move to the next instructional stage before the strategy has been memorized may be counterproductive.

TROUBLESHOOTING

If students have difficulty memorizing the steps of the remembering system, you may want to try to use a chaining technique to assist them. Here, one person says all but the last step of the strategy. The student is required to provide this last step. Next, provide all but the last two steps of the strategy. The student then says the last two steps. You progressively work backward until the student can name all the steps. If the student has trouble remembering a single step, a similar chaining technique can be used. One person says the first word or two of the step, and then the student who is struggling to memorize the steps of the strategy is prompted to say the remaining words that comprise that step.

Planning for Strategy Practice

10

GOAL: To develop a plan for providing practice experiences to students that will lead to their appropriate use of strategies to successfully complete tasks.

ORIENTATION

Keep in mind that practice lessons should not focus only on prompting the student to acquire strategy steps; practice should also address promoting successful learning and performance. That is, the strategy being taught should be thought of as the vehicle to be used to help both teacher and student understand success on a task. Practice must be organized to (a) promote an understanding of the *application* of the strategy so that the strategy can be used as a self-instructional guide or mediational tool that both the teacher and students can use to guide and monitor learning and (b) teach students how to successfully meet the demands that they face across school and out of school settings.

Four steps can help in the development of an appropriate plan for practice. First, the teacher should make a decision regarding the type of practice that best matches what students must learn. Second, the teacher should make a decision regarding the level of guidance or help to be provided to students during the practice activities. Third, the teacher should make a decision regarding the types of materials and/or activities that will be used for practice. And fourth, the teacher should make decisions regarding performance criteria to be used for instructional decision making, including changes in practice and feedback.

These four steps of the planning process and how a teacher might begin to think about arranging successful practice experiences using them will be discussed in this chapter. Although these areas are referred to as steps, their sequence of implementation is not critical. All four steps, however, should be completed before the planning process concludes. As the planning process is described, basic types of practice related to strategy learning will be briefly explained; the remaining three steps of planning strategy practice will be presented in some detail. The four chapters that follow this chapter will provide more detailed explanations of the basic types of strategy practice and related planning decisions.

PLANNING PROCEDURES

Step 1: Select Type of Practice

As students move into the practice stages of strategy acquisition and generalization that are described in the following chapters, they should be able to recall and explain each of the steps of the strategy. The describe, model, and verbal elaboration and rehearsal stages of strategies instruction should promote this level of competence. The practice stages that follow must focus on promoting competence in application of the strategy.

One of the first teacher decisions that must be made about practice is what the student must know about application of the strategy. All practice can be thought of as instruction in the features of a task, how to recognize those features, and how to use these features to make decisions about the best way to complete the task. Therefore, the type of practice that is selected must take into consideration what the student needs to learn about tasks and the order in which this information should be learned.

Based on observations of many students learning strategies, students appear to need to learn five processes associated with learning to apply a strategy to a task. First, they must learn how to physically or procedurally go through the motions of applying the strategy on very simple tasks for which the probability of success is quite high. At this point students must learn to associate what they have only verbalized and observed with the actions that must be performed to complete a task. Second, students must learn how to explain how they think during each step of the strategy process and to consider alternatives as each step of the strategy is applied. This process often requires the teacher to guide students in how they think. For example, the teacher might repeat modeling thinking and ask the students to describe how they are thinking and why. Third, students should learn to see the task from different perspectives. Specifically, they must have opportunities to talk about the task with peers so that additional insights and ways of thinking about completing the task can be considered and evaluated. Fourth, students must learn how to independently apply the strategy to complete tasks in a fluent manner. Fifth, students must learn how to critically evaluate features of tasks characteristic of real-life settings and how to apply the strategy to them. Some students may already have knowledge related to how to apply the strategy across these types of practice conditions. Many students will not.

The types of practice described above can be organized into four different conditions: (1) teacher-assisted practice, (2) peer-assisted practice, (3) self-mediated practice, and (4) advanced practice. In successive order, these practice conditions provide a continuum for promoting student strategy learning. The decision that must be made in this step of the planning process is which practice condition to select, and when. Many students who have significant difficulties completing the types of tasks for which a certain strategy is appropriate will need to begin with the first practice condition and proceed through the others in order. Other students may be able to skip some of these types of practice. Information about each of these conditions is presented below so that a decision can be made regarding selection of the most appropriate practice conditions for individual students. Each is presented in greater detail in the chapters that follow.

Teacher-Assisted Practice

Initial practice begins with the teacher playing a major role in assisting student learning. The teacher-assisted practice condition focuses on the teacher prompting students to apply the strategy procedures to a task and then teaching the student to be reflective in thinking about and performing the strategy. There are two phases to teacher-assisted practice: procedural practice and reflective practice.

In *procedural practice* the teacher guides students' involvement in practice activities in a manner that focuses their attention on mastering the more overt or procedural aspects of the strategy. The goal here is to help the student understand how the strategy is applied so that in later stages of practice both teacher and student can use the strategy framework to discuss successful completion of the task. This type of practice is a logical extension of the verbal practice stage in that students are now prompted to actually perform the strategy on simple tasks rather than merely talk about the strategy. The teacher should select practice materials and activities with which the strategy can be easily applied and that will enable students to become confident and motivated.

Implementation of *reflective practice* involves shifting the emphasis of practice from the overt and behavioral aspects of strategy implementation to an emphasis on appropriate ways to think about the task and implementation of the strategy. In this type of practice, the teacher arranges experiences in which she or he prompts students to think about the cognitive actions associated with each aspect of the strategy. The teacher models and remodels both the cognitive and physical actions that might be required and then prompts students to do the same as they practice applying the strategy to complete tasks. The teacher should gradually increase the difficulty of the practice materials and activities and vary them so that students have an opportunity to see and hear how the teacher thinks about using the strategy in those situations.

Peer-Assisted Practice

Peer-assisted practice can be used to aid the process of transferring responsibility for mediation of the strategy from teacher to student. Students may learn as much from peers as they do from the teacher regarding how a strategy can be used. Thus, students should interact among themselves when practicing a strategy both prior to and in conjunction with implementation of independent practice activities. This allows students to translate the strategy into their own language and to experiment with how to apply the strategy. Prompting dialogue among students about how the strategy is used may significantly enhance their understanding of the strategy and how it can be used. Peer-assisted practice includes instructional–learning arrangements and activities often referred to as cooperative learning or peer tutoring. Students participating in peer-assisted practice activities will require the teacher to monitor the accuracy and appropriateness of their adaptations of the strategy. For this to be successful, the teacher must plan how to promote successful peer interactions.

Self-Mediated Practice

The primary purpose of self-mediated practice is to provide students with opportunities to build fluency in independently responding to a task using a strategy. During this process, both the overt and covert behaviors associated with using the strategy are performed automatically and quickly. Students should have little need for teacher cues and prompts in the nature of the strategy at this point. Feedback, however, must become very individualized, with the student playing a major role in checking for errors, correcting errors, and generating alternatives. The materials and activities used during this practice condition are typically selected to (a) gradually present increasingly difficult challenges to students; (b) allow for enough errors to enable correction, feedback, and some teacher instruction; and (c) ensure a degree of success that is sufficient to keep students successful and motivated in efforts to learn the strategy.

Advanced Practice

The focus of the advanced practice condition is on teaching the student how to recognize specific features of real-world tasks calling for the strategy and to apply the strategy to similar tasks. These include tasks associated with the regular content area classroom and those from settings outside school (e.g., home, community, work). Activities during the advanced practice condition may incorporate all of the previously mentioned practice conditions. The focus, however, will be on transfer of the strategy.

Step 2: Select Practice Materials and Activities

When students are practicing the strategy, provide them with different types of materials and tasks. Initial practice materials and activities should present opportunities for the student to learn the strategy while controlling for the nature of the content. To facilitate (and help ensure) content learning when the strategy is new, the content should not be too complex. As students learn the strategy, the practice activities should gradually make more content learning demands on the student.

In general, the types of materials and activities selected for use in practice depend on the type of practice to be engaged in by students. The specific nature of these materials and how they relate to each type of practice will be discussed in detail in each of the following chapters related to practice. Across the types of practice there are four major considerations for adapting or controlling for the nature of practice materials: quantity of information, duration of the task, complexity of the task, and reading level.

Quantity of Information

For some tasks it is important to control how much information the student will be expected to learn. For example, if the student must learn how to identify major concepts in a text, initial practice attempts may include presenting the student with text selections that include no more than, say, five concepts in each practice activity.

Duration of the Task

Sometimes controlling a task for practice may require reducing the length of the task. For example, in teaching a student how to take notes, initial practice attempts may be based on short 5-minute lectures. As the student learns the strategy and can easily take notes on the 5-minute segments, the length of the lectures can be increased until they approximate a typical classroom lecture length.

Complexity of the Task

Many tasks are so complex that initial practice attempts may be most successful when the task is simplified, so that the strategy is easily used to successfully complete the task. The student must find the strategy working on the task in order to become motivated and confident in using it. The complexity of the task can, however, be gradually increased as the strategy is mastered. For example, in teaching a student the Paraphrasing Strategy, the initial practice activities may include paragraphs in which the main idea is clearly stated. However, as practice continues the materials should include paragraphs in which the main idea is embedded or not obviously stated.

Reading Level

The teacher can control the nature of the practice materials by using materials that are selected from lower grade levels than the current ability of the student. A student in the 10th grade but reading at a 5th-grade level may be given a 4th- or 5th-grade textbook or a high school textbook written at that level to use when practicing the strategy. Again, as the strategy is learned, the materials used for practice should begin to approximate those that are associated with the task in the real world (i.e., the student's actual 10th-grade textbooks).

Students' initial attempts at using a strategy on more difficult or different materials, regardless of the practice condition, may initially require intensive assistance from the teacher. Teacher assistance should gradually shift to providing assistance in a more intermittent fashion. The teacher's role should phase from instructor to facilitator to coach. Decisions related to how much assistance should be provided to students during practice are discussed in the next section.

Step 3: Select Help Level

After the type of practice and the materials for the practice have been selected, the next decision in the planning process occurs both before and during implementation of practice activities. The teacher must determine how much and what type of help to provide to students during practice to promote their progress in learning. To the student, help can be thought of as the degree or level of teacher assistance that is provided in order for the student to respond in a manner that contributes to successful completion of the task or to respond in a manner that contributes to the completion of a step in the overall process of completing the task.

In general a task using very controlled materials will require less assistance than a task using more grade-appropriate materials. The decision on the degree of help to be provided by the teacher must be made in relation to the materials and situation in which they are being used. In making decisions about the amount and type of teacher assistance during practice, the following factors should be taken into consideration:

- The more limited the guidance and assistance that is provided to the student, the greater is the responsibility that must be assumed by the student for learning and task completion.

- The greater the guidance and assistance that is provided to the student, the more limited is the responsibility the student must assume for learning and task completion.

- The more limited the guidance and assistance that is provided and maintained by the teacher, especially in the early stages of learning, the less likely it will be for the student to learn how to assume responsibility for independent learning and performance.

- The greater the guidance and assistance provided by the teacher in the early stages of learning (and then gradually reduced as the student becomes more proficient), the more likely it will be for the student to learn to assume responsibility for independent learning and performance.

The teacher must make decisions about the type and level of guidance to use that will teach the student how to assume responsibility for independent learning and task completion across time and a variety of circumstances, situations, settings, and materials. Such guidance and assistance is called mediation. *Mediation* is defined as the process of intervening or interceding between the learner and the to-be-learned information in order to induce learning or an appropriate response. The teacher can assist and guide students in a manner that will mediate their learning or will prompt them to self-mediate learning more effectively. The process of mediation involves both the procedural and reflective aspects of learning and performance.

The following is a list of various levels of help and a description of each. They are ordered by degree of teacher guidance. As you will notice, the first three help levels focus on providing assistance in applying the strategy and the last three levels focus on helping the student understand the task so that the strategy can be applied.

6. *Student responds when teacher guides student in response.* This is the highest level of assistance and mediation provided by the teacher. At this level, guidance is intensive. The teacher may talk the student through the task and cue and prompt the student to perform each step or aspect of the strategy. At key points, the teacher may completely model the strategy and perform the task and then ask the student to repeat the process.

5. *Student responds when strategy is modeled.* Once the student understands and can perform the essential components of the strategy, the teacher reduces the intensity of mediation and begins to observe the student's performance. The teacher attempts to identify which aspects of the strategy are particularly troublesome for the student. At this point, the teacher models the strategy to show the student how it is applied. If modeling does not result in understanding, the teacher may return to intensive describing, prompting, and cueing.

4. *Student responds when strategy is elicited/suggested.* This level of mediation is provided when the student demonstrates understanding of the strategy and applies it, but appears to have difficulty recognizing the features of tasks or situations in which to apply the strategy or a strategy step. The focus of assistance is on prompting and cueing application of major sections of the strategy or the whole strategy. The student does not, however, need intensive cueing to perform the strategy.

3. *Student responds when task is segmented/reexplained.* The teacher can move to this level of mediation when the student appears to understand the strategy and its application, but the tasks on which the strategy is to be applied become difficult or unique. As practice shifts to different materials or activities, the student may understand the strategy and know that the strategy is appropriate for the task, but may need help understanding the task and its relationship to the strategy.

2. *Student responds with clarification/questions answered.* The teacher moves to this level of assistance when the student is applying the strategy to appropriate tasks on a regular basis. The focus of assistance is on answering questions and providing feedback to the student's attempts to apply the strategy to tasks.

1. *Student responds with little or no mediation or assistance.* The final level of mediation involves allowing the student to work on tasks on an independent level. Little or no assistance is given to the student. This level of mediation is used for promoting fluency and confidence and is the last level of assistance that is provided before there is a shift in practice conditions. This level is also the level that is used for testing and evaluating mastery.

In general the amount of teacher mediation and guidance moves from intensive assistance to intermittent assistance. In the early stages of learning the strategy, students who attempt to perform the strategy independently are likely to experience a high rate of failure and frustration. Therefore, students should receive intensive teacher mediation that includes specific guidance, cueing, and feedback. The teacher frequently models and remodels the specific behaviors associated with using the strategy and provides ample prompts and cues to mediate use of the strategy to ensure that here is a low rate of incorrect response from students. When difficulties in applying the strategy arise, the teacher should discuss the difficulties and provide feedback. However, as students begin to assume more responsibility for mediating the use of the strategy themselves, teacher mediation and assistance should become more intermittent. During these practice activities, the prompts and cues provided during the earlier attempts to use the strategy are gradually faded until students are able to perform the strategy independently.

Step 4: Determine Performance Criteria

As students move through practice exercises, the teacher should have a clear idea of the performance criteria that are to be used to make instructional decisions. These performance criteria indicate the level of performance to be expected as a standard for measuring progress and evaluating mastery during each type of practice.

There are two areas in which criteria need to be established. The first area is the student's strategic performance. Strategic performance is the degree to which the student correctly performs the steps of the strategy. It can be thought of as a process measure or a measure of student mediation. The second area for which criteria should be established is the student's outcome performance. Outcome performance concerns the results of application of a strategy to a task. It is the degree to which the strategy is used by the student in meeting task demands.

Establishing Criteria for Strategic Performance

The criteria for mastery that are established for evaluating strategic performance should address two types of information. First, is the student correctly, or accurately, performing the strategy? Because your goal is for students to correctly perform the strategy to help complete a task, you will need to establish a minimal level of acceptable performance using the strategy steps. Here you are concerned with what the student does when performing the strategy (e.g., is she correctly using the strategy steps?), not with the results of the behavior (e.g., did comprehension increase?). For example, the mastery criteria for strategic performance related to the application of the prewriting portion of the DEFENDS Writing Strategy might include the generation of an organizer form that indicates an established position, two different reasons for the position, and three details per reason.

The second type of strategic performance information that can be used in establishing criteria relates to fluency. Fluency concerns the *speed* or the level of *automaticity* at which the strategy is performed correctly. Students will not only need to master correct use of the DEFENDS Writing Strategy; they will also need to master its fluent application. As a result, students learning an expository writing strategy need to master the pre-writing processes associated with the strategy, and they must do them quickly and automatically.

Establishing Criteria for Outcome Performance

Outcome performance is measured by the results or products generated when the strategy is used to complete tasks. The result of using the Paragraph Writing Strategy might be a well-organized paragraph that clearly establishes and then explains the writer's position. Mastery levels here might be the production of a paragraph that contains a minimum of 7 sentences including an opening sentence that establishes a position, a sentence telling the most important reason why the writer has taken a specific position, one sentence for each elaboration explaining the reason, and so forth.

To establish mastery criteria for outcome performance, think about the quality of the product. How good does it need to be? Consider the setting demands that the strategy was designed to address. The mastery levels should be set at either the same levels as those found in the criterion environment or at slightly higher levels.

PUTTING PRACTICE IN PERSPECTIVE

In summary, conceptualizing how practice activities will be implemented involves four major instructional decisions. First, the type of practice must be selected as practice is initiated or a shift to a different type of practice is being considered. Second, the materials or conditions surrounding the practice must be selected such that the student will be able to acquire the essential elements of the strategy while building confidence and motivation. Third, the teacher must decide how much assistance or help will be provided to the student so strategy acquisition and independence will be maximized. And fourth, the criteria for strategic performance and outcome performance should be identified so that both the teacher and the student know the standards for instructional decisions and mastery of the strategy.

Teacher-Assisted Practice

GOAL: To guide students in their practice attempts so as to enable them to engage in the procedural and reflective aspects of accurate strategy performance.

ORIENTATION

In teacher-assisted practice the teacher aids the student in strategy implementation and encourages the student to focus attention on mastering both overt and covert strategy behaviors.

There are two phases of teacher-assisted practice. The first phase is focused on providing students with procedural practice. *Procedural practice* involves prompting and guiding students to practice the more overt or behavioral aspects of the strategy. The second phase of teacher-assisted practice focuses on providing students with reflective practice. *Reflective practice* involves prompting and guiding students to practice, becoming aware of the more covert or cognitive aspects of strategy performance. Many reflective practice activities involve teacher-directed instruction to students working in groups. The two phases of teacher-assisted practice are more thoroughly described in the following sections.

PREPARATION

Preparations for procedural and reflective practice activities involve (a) identifying materials that are conducive to providing a slight challenge to students while at the same time not being so difficult as to cause frustration and failure, and (b) selecting criteria for evaluating strategic performance and outcomes. When preparing materials and activities to be used when students are practicing the new strategy for the first few times, remember that the subject matter of the materials should be simple and familiar to students as well as free of obstacles that could make the strategy difficult to perform. Once students are able to independently and fluently use the strategy on a relatively easy level, select materials that present a slightly greater challenge to them.

PROCEDURES

The specific instructional procedures used during the teacher-mediated stage of instruction are described in two sections. The first section (Phase I) describes the procedures used when providing intensive teacher mediation. The second section (Phase II) addresses procedures used when providing intermittent teacher mediation.

Phase I: Procedural Practice

The first time students actually perform a strategy, you will need to provide intensive mediation in forms such as ample prompts, cues, and directive feedback. Materials should be carefully chosen to control for difficulty. Your goal is to assure that students are correctly performing the strategy steps. Thus, emphasis here is on developing accuracy at using the strategy, not fluency.

Time Considerations

In most cases, intensive teacher mediation may be necessary for only one to two applications of a new strategy (e.g., writing one to two essays for the Paragraph Writing Strategy; reading one to two 400-word passages for the Paraphrasing Strategy). Naturally, these time lines will vary, depending on the characteristics of your students, the relative sophistication of the strategy you are teaching, and the difficulty of the materials being used.

Procedures for Intensive Teacher Mediation

Because intensive mediation is provided by you during this phase of instruction, you should inform students during the advance organizer that the purpose of this first practice attempt is for them to learn to apply the strategy steps accurately—not quickly (that will come later). Tell students that you will be carefully guiding them as they perform the strategy. Ask them not to get ahead of you since you will be pointing out important things to think about as they perform each part of the strategy.

You may find it effective to write the strategy steps on the board or overhead projector, label them as "what to do" steps, and next to these, provide categories titled "when" and "what to think." Then as students perform the strategy, point to the strategy step, cue students to perform it, and note what they should be thinking as they do it. This procedure tends to make critical overt and covert behaviors very explicit for students. The more explicit you are, the better students will master the strategy.

After providing the advance organizer, begin prompting students as they perform the strategy. Be sure to prompt cognitive processes as well as overt steps. Model and remodel specific behaviors as necessary. Continue guiding students as they perform the strategy until they have completed the procedure.

Instructional Decisions

When should I begin to fade prompts? When do I begin using intermittent teacher mediation? As a general rule, you should not fade prompts during students' first practice attempts at using the new strategy. The entire application should be heavily laden with your guidance in performing both overt and covert behaviors. Once students, given your prompts, are able to correctly perform the overt steps of the strategy, then they are ready to begin assuming more responsibility for mediation.

Should I let the faster students move ahead of me? During this initial practice attempt, do not succumb to the temptation to allow students to independently perform the strategy. You may feel that it is okay for faster students to "get ahead of you," but allowing them to do so can be counterproductive. This practice may reinforce students' beliefs that the strategy is a simple procedure. Allowing them to get ahead of you essentially undermines the importance of the cognitive processes, creates a sense of false security on the students' part, and produces a situation that is conducive to practicing incorrect behaviors.

Troubleshooting

What should I do if some of the students quickly learn to use the strategy while others need a lot more assistance? You have three choices here. You can subgroup your students (e.g., fast group, slow group) and work with them separately on the strategy, allowing the faster group to work on something else as you work with the slower group, or the faster students can work as instructional aides with the slower students. This last option is probably the best. In fact, mixing those who have learned the strategy quickly with those who need more assistance is the ideal form of grouping. Students who need assistance typically respond positively to this form of assistance, and "faster" students learn the strategy more thoroughly when assisting others in its use.

What should I do if a student is not able to perform the strategy, even with extensive guidance? The most common reason students are unable to perform a new strategy even with extensive guidance is that the prerequisite skills associated with performing the strategy have not been sufficiently mastered by the student. For example, to perform the Paraphrasing Strategy, students should read independently and at least at the 4th-grade level. You may need to suspend strategy instruction in order to extensively review or teach prerequisite skills.

Phase II: Reflective Practice

The purpose of this phase is to shift the responsibility for mediating use of the strategy to the students. Here, you will be gradually fading the extent to which you provide prompts. Feedback will still be directive.

Time Considerations

Most students require this form of instruction for two to five practice applications of the strategy. The characteristics of your students, the relative sophistication of the strategy you are teaching, and the difficulty of the stimulus materials used will naturally affect the amount of time required.

Procedures for Intermittent Teacher Mediation

During this phase of instruction, the nature of your mediation will shift from mediating the use of the strategy to mediating students' mediation. That is, the prompts you provide shift from cueing students on what to do next to cueing them to *think about* what to do next. Inform students during the advance organizer for this phase of instruction that they are beginning a new phase of controlled practice. Explicitly tell them that, before, you had been the person primarily responsible for thinking about what needs to happen next when performing the strategy. Now they will be learning to take control of these processes. Tell them that you will be gradually fading prompts and cues so that by the end of this phase of controlled practice, they will be able to perform the strategy without much help from you. Tell them that you will be cueing them less about what to do and more about what to think.

Instructional Decisions

When will I know when it is time to begin providing peer-mediated practice activities? Students are ready to practice the strategy in a cooperative format when they are performing the strategy accurately with little help from you. Attaining accuracy, not necessarily fluency, is the key consideration during this phase of practice.

Troubleshooting

What should I do if a student is not able to perform the strategy when I fade prompts? It is not unusual for students with learning disabilities (LD) to be able to perform the strategy when someone else is mediating the process but to be at a loss when expected to begin mediating the process themselves. There are several techniques you can use to circumvent this problem:

- Fade your cues more gradually. There may have been too big a leap between your mediating the strategic process and turning over the responsibility to the student.

- Determine whether the student comprehends the strategy. Although students should have completed the verbal rehearsal stage of instruction (where the emphasis is on facilitating comprehension of the strategy) before beginning the controlled practice stage, some students may still not understand that the strategy is actually a problem-solving process, as opposed to a collection of good things to do. You may need to provide the students with more opportunities for verbally elaborating on the strategic process.

- Reiterate the role of self-instruction. Although you have been extensively modeling covert problem solving processes by thinking out loud, some students may have missed the point or not realized that what you were modeling is exactly what you expect them to learn to do when performing the strategy. In subsequent practice attempts, cue students to think out loud themselves (use probing questions to instigate thoughts if you need to) as they perform the strategy.

Peer-Mediated
Practice

GOAL: To enable students to become more effective strategy users by facilitating their opportunities to learn how others use the strategy and by providing opportunities to build fluency.

ORIENTATION

Mastering use of a new strategy requires that students both perform the overt procedures associated with using the strategy and mediate the strategic process. There are several reasons why you should provide students with peer-mediated practice to guide mastery. Students learn how others use and think about the strategy, which serves as both a model and an impetus to reflect on their own practice. By interacting with peers as they use the strategy, students learn about many of the subtleties involved in its use that you may not address. Sometimes fellow students are able to more effectively express difficult strategy concepts than when these concepts are explained by you; they share a common novice perspective that you lack. Also, peers may be able to motivate reluctant learners by modeling their enthusiasm for using the strategy and expressing the valuing of it.

Use of peer-mediated practice activities also provides students with a different source of mediation. In these situations students cue and prompt each other's strategic behaviors. The fact that peer-mediated practice activities tend to be enjoyed by students is an added benefit. Working together to solve problems can be more fun than working alone. (In an orderly classroom fun will not outweigh learning.) Students often gain a better understanding of the strategic processes themselves and are better able to use them as a result of cueing and prompting other students' strategic behaviors.

Remember, the purpose of using peer-mediated activities is not necessarily to teach new skills, but rather to provide students with opportunities to broaden their expertise at using skills previously learned and to practice performing the new skills in order to build proficiency or fluency.

GENERAL CONSIDERATIONS FOR PREPARATION

Preparing for this instructional stage involves (a) identifying materials and contexts that are conducive to students working together to apply the strategy and (b) designing activities for group practice.

As with other phases of initial practice, select materials that address a subject matter that will be familiar to all students in the group and are free of obstacles that could make the strategy difficult to perform (e.g., complex concepts). When preparing materials for activities used during advanced practice activities, use materials similar to those found in students' content-area classrooms.

The activities selected should be structured to allow ample opportunity for all to interact. See Johnson, Johnson, and Holubec (1988) or Kagan (1992) for important suggestions on how to effectively structure cooperative activities. For a peer-mediated activity to practice the Paraphrasing Strategy, you might divide your class into small groups and then provide each with a set of six paragraphs; then, ask each group to read each paragraph and discuss among themselves to determine the best paraphrases.

TIME CONSIDERATIONS

The amount of time required to complete a peer-mediated practice activity will vary, depending on the nature of the task and the strategy and the proficiency of members of the group. With strategies that take more time to perform, you may have to design peer-mediated activities that are used over a period of a few days. Students might spend approximately 20 minutes per day over a 2- to 3-day period. Small groups might work together for 10 to 15 minutes one day to perform the prewriting aspects of the strategy and produce the rough draft with initial edits on the following day. The final version would then be completed the following day.

PROCEDURES

Three different sets of procedures for peer-mediated practice are presented below. The first set includes activities in which students practice analyzing materials. This type of practice activity can be used throughout the various stages of learning a new strategy. This type of activity can also be used much later in the learning process, when students are learning to use the strategy on materials found in regular classroom settings.

The second type of activity with which peer-mediated procedures can be used is when the team applies the strategy with practice materials. Like those described above, this type of peer-mediated activity is appropriately used both early in the learning process when relatively easy materials are used and when students have nearly mastered the strategy and are using relatively challenging materials. There are two approaches you can use. One is to design the activity in a manner that allows each student to be responsible for a specific component of the strategy so that the result of using the strategy is dependent on each individual student's contribution to the process. In the second approach, team members perform the entire strategy themselves when using the same materials, but they help each other think through each of the various steps and then give each other feedback.

The third type of peer-mediated practice activity should be reserved for the latter stages of mastering the strategy. Here, students work in teams to both analyze novel stimulus materials and generate adaptations in the strategy to meet new setting demands. These procedures differ significantly from those addressed here; they will be addressed later in this book.

Peer-Mediated Procedures for Practice Involving Analyzing Materials

1. *Decide membership for student groups.* Keep group sizes small enough for all to participate (i.e., 5 to 6 maximum). Varying membership by knowledge about strategies and current abilities in the area related to the new strategy may be helpful. See Johnson et al. (1988) for tips on organizing small groups.

2. *Provide an advance organizer.* Explain to students that they will be working in small groups and that the primary goals will be to (a) help each other become experts at using the strategy and (b) learn how others think when they use it. Tell the students that the activity has two parts. Their first task is to analyze the materials they will be using and to talk about how the strategy can be used to perform the task. Second, they are to discuss and answer questions you will give them.

3. *Have students analyze materials.* Provide each group with enough copies of the materials to be used. Tell the students what you want them to do. Tell them that their first task is to analyze the stimulus material and discuss among themselves about how the strategy can be used with the materials. Each group should record ideas generated in the group. Model for the students what you want them to do. Model how you analyze the materials, thinking aloud as you do it. Be sure to also model how you record your ideas. Structure requirements for those groups likely to produce a minimum amount of responses. You can structure requirements by, for example, indicating a minimum number of specific types of responses students are to generate. When students are to analyze reading materials prior to using the Paraphrasing Strategy, you might say:

> *Take a look at this book chapter. You need to look it over and come up with answers to the following questions:*
>
> - *Can the title of the chapter be paraphrased? Does it contain enough information to allow you to paraphrase it? Why or why not?*
>
> - *Are there any organizers or objectives anywhere in this chapter that can be paraphrased?*
>
> - *Which of the visual aids look like they contain enough information to paraphrase?*

- *Which paragraphs might be too short to paraphrase?*
- *Which paragraphs look like they are too long to paraphrase?*

4. *Have teams compare findings.* Once students have finished analyzing the materials, have each group summarize their findings for other groups working on the same stimulus materials.

5. *Provide closure.* Once the teams have shared the results of their findings with each other, you should provide closure to the activity by (a) summarizing their findings regarding analyzing the materials, (b) reviewing the goal of learning how others view and think about using the strategy, and (c) providing feedback with regard to how well students worked in their groups. You should then (d) introduce the next activity, which, in many cases, will be practice at performing the strategy.

Peer-Mediated Procedures for Practice When A Team Performs the Strategy Together

At this stage of practice, each team member is responsible for performing a specific component of the process.

1. *Provide an advance organizer.* Inform students that they will be working in small groups to practice using the strategy together. Tell them that each member of the team will perform an important part of the strategy. When finished, team members will have worked together to help each other become experts at using the strategy. Inform them that the activity includes three tasks. Their first task is to analyze the material and talk about how the strategy can be used to perform the task. Second, individual students are to perform one part of the strategy, but others may help them as needed. Encourage students to think aloud when they perform their part of the strategy. Last, after the strategy has been used, students are to discuss and answer questions you will give them. Be sure to explicitly communicate that the goals of the activity are to (a) learn how others think when they use the strategy, as well as what they think about the strategy; (b) become more effective at using the strategy individually; and (c) help their team members become more effective strategy users.

2. *Assign roles to each student.* In this type of a cooperative learning activity, different students should have different roles, each of which is vital to the success of the activity. Assign each student in the group the responsibility of performing specific steps in the strategy. For example, when providing peer-mediated practice using the DEFENDS Writing Strategy, you might say:

> Now I'm going to assign each of you a specific job for when you do this strategy together. Bill, it will be your job to make sure the first step in the strategy, "Decide on audience, goals, and position," gets done effectively. You'll need to get everyone's input on what the position will be, but you make sure than an exact position is established by your group, and you'll need to write it on the organizer form.
>
> Jolene, it will be your job to get the group to do the second step of the strategy, "Estimate main ideas and details." You need to get everyone's ideas on these, and have the group help decide which you should list on the organizer form.
>
> Sandra, it will be your job to have your team deal with the third step of the strategy. . . .

3. *Tell and model specific instructions.* Instruct students in what is expected of them when practicing the strategy as a team. Model how a student might perform a specific role.

4. *Have students perform their roles when practicing the strategy.* You should closely monitor the interaction between students to ensure that each of the team members is actively participating and that they are all encouraging and helping each other.

5. *Have students evaluate their own performance.* Encourage students to first evaluate performance outcomes (e.g., use the score sheet and evaluate their own essay). Next, have them evaluate strategic functioning (to what degree did members of this group apply each step of the strategy?). Checklists of critical behaviors associated with performing the strategy are effective when evaluating strategic functioning.

6. *Promote student dialogue about how the strategy was used.* Once students have made their individual contributions to performing the strategy, encourage them to discuss the critical features of the problem solving process. Sample prompt question include:

- How well did the strategy work on this material?

- What was the easiest part of performing the strategy? Why was it so easy?

- What was the hardest part of performing the strategy? Why?

- How did different students in your group use the strategy differently than the way you usually do it?

7. *Have groups share the results of the activity with other teams.* Each group shares with the other groups the results of its use of the strategy and discusses with them the answers to the questions discussed above.

8. *Provide teacher-directed closure.* Provide closure to the activity by (a) reviewing the goals of the activity and discussing the degree to which the goals were met, (b) summarizing key points expressed by students when they were discussing the strategy among themselves, and (c) providing feedback with regard to how well students worked in their teams.

Peer-Mediated Procedures for Practice Performing the Strategy When Each Team Member Performs the Entire Strategy

At this stage of practice, peers help each other think through each of the various steps and provide reinforcement and feedback.

1. *Provide an advance organizer.* Inform students that they will be practicing using the strategy individually while receiving help from team members, if needed. Each member of the team will have a specific job that will help other team members become experts at using the strategy independently. Each member will have to analyze the materials to figure out how the strategy can be used to perform the task. Then, each member will apply the strategy. Afterward, team members will work together to evaluate each other's work and give feedback and reinforcement as well as discuss how the strategy was used. Tell students that each member of the team will have the important job of helping the team do as well as possible.

2. *Assign "helper" roles to each student.* Although each student in the team will be performing the strategy independently, each should have a role in the overall team process. Although you may wish to create your own, a set of "helper" roles are suggested below.

Start/Ender: This person is responsible for assuring that everyone understands the instructions. Responsibilities also include quickly reviewing the steps to the strategy with team members and facilitating the process of evaluating performance outcomes.

Prompter: This student is responsible for prompting others in the group to perform each step of the strategy as the previous step is completed. Prompters quickly review what to do in the upcoming step and why it is important. Following the prompt, students perform the step to the strategy.

Facilitator: This person is responsible for facilitating dialogue as the students discuss how the strategy was used, what aspects were easiest to perform, etc.

Presenter: The presenter is responsible for sharing the results of the team's performance outcomes and dialogue.

3. *Tell and model specific instructions.* To introduce the roles to students for the first time, construct a chart or bulletin board that lists the various responsibilities of each. In addition, it is a good idea to provide students with a cue card that summarizes these roles. You should also model the various responsibilities by role-playing.

To model the responsibilities of helper roles, form a team that includes you as a student. Tell students to observe how you perform each role. For example, review the responsibilities of the starter/ender role and then model those behaviors. After modeling the behaviors, review the responsibilities by asking students to tell what you did as the starter/ender. Follow this process for each role.

4. *Have students perform their roles when practicing the strategy.* As students use this activity for the first time, closely monitor them and provide extensive prompts and reinforcement to help them perform their roles effectively.

5. *Have students evaluate each other's performance and provide feedback.*

6. *Prompt student dialogue about how the strategy was used.*

7. *Provide teacher-directed closure.* When providing closure to the lesson, (a) review the goals of the activity and discuss the degree to which the goals were met, (b) summarize key points expressed by students when they were helping each other or explaining the strategy, and (c) provide feedback regarding how well students performed the strategies.

INSTRUCTIONAL DECISIONS

There are many ways to use peer-mediated learning activities. You may wish to arrange a situation whereby groups are competing with each other but individuals within the group are cooperating. Or, groups can evaluate the products of other groups. Having students work in pairs to perform the strategy, in lieu of groups, can also be effective. Each member of the group could perform the strategy while attaining help from other group members. Regardless of the way you arrange the peer-mediated practice activity, you should structure opportunities for students to carry on dialogue about the strategy. Information about some specific decisions you will likely need to make is provided below.

When should I use peer-mediated practice activities? There are a number of appropriate times throughout the process of teaching a new strategy to use peer-mediated practice activities:

- following teacher-mediated practice during the initial stages of learning the strategy

- when students are learning to apply the strategy to tasks that begin to approximate those found in the regular classroom setting

- when students are learning to adapt the strategy to meet different setting demands

- when students, as a whole, seem to be losing interest

- when students are learning to make decisions with regard to when to use the strategy and when it is not appropriate

How should materials and practice tasks be designed when using peer-mediated activities? The difficulty level of materials used when providing practice activities will vary, depending in part on the point to which students have mastered the strategy. When students are in the early stages of learning the new strategy, the difficulty of the materials should be relatively similar to those used when you are providing teacher-mediated practice. Later, once students have become relatively facile at using the strategy, you can use peer-mediated activities to introduce slightly more challenging tasks and ask students to work together to use the strategy when addressing these tasks.

Should mastery levels of strategy performance be different when peer-mediated activities are used? Remember, effective strategy behaviors encompass two types of performance. The first concerns mastery levels of strategic functioning, or the degree to which students are actually correctly performing the strategy steps. The second concerns the results of these behaviors or mastery levels of performance outcomes. Mastery levels for each of these measures should be the same as those used when providing teacher-mediated practice activities.

How many peer-mediated practice activities should I provide? There are no clear-cut rules that specify the extent to which peer-mediated activities should be used. You will need to use your own judgment in making this decision.

How much teacher involvement should I provide when using peer-mediated activities? Remember that peer-mediated practice is a time for students to learn more from each other than from you. Your primary role is to design and structure activities in a manner that promotes students' interaction with each other as they practice the strategy. Your involvement during these activities should be related to prompting, encouraging, and reinforcing student interactions. If students seek your help in performing specific aspects of the strategy (e.g., "We don't know how to do this. What do we do now?"), prompt them to analyze the situation and identify the appropriate behaviors rather than simply telling them what to do. Allow students to make mistakes as well as problem solve.

How large should groups be? Effective cooperative groups typically include four to five members. Using three students per group often results in a dyad and an outsider. (See Simel, 1950, for an interesting discussion suggesting that all group interactions can ultimately be dyadic.) Groups larger than five tend to make for reduced opportunities for participation.

How should students be assigned to groups? The groups should be heterogeneous so that students with higher skills are working with those with less skills. Try to have an "encouraging" student in each group who will model positive behaviors. Active "talkers" should also be spread around to avoid having a group of "nontalkers" sitting around waiting for some other member of the group to begin the discussion.

Self-Mediated Practice

GOAL: To enable students to perform strategies accurately and fluently without assistance
from others.

DEFINITIONS

Mediation: The process of regulating use of the strategy (deciding
whether the strategy is needed to complete a task, regulating behaviors as
the strategy is applied, monitoring, assessing, and reinforcing).

Self-Mediation: The individual student independently regulates use of
the strategy, assesses outcomes, provides self with feedback and reinforcement. The student is responsible for both overt and covert strategic
behaviors.

ORIENTATION

Self-mediated practice enables students to accurately and fluently perform the strategy. During this stage of instruction, students become so
familiar with performing the strategy that much of it becomes internal-
ized processes performed automatically and quickly. You may, only on

occasion, need to provide cues, prompts, reinforcement, and feedback; self-mediated practice is appropriate only for those students who can perform the strategy accurately with little help from you or others.

PREPARATION
Preparing Materials and Practice Tasks

As students become more adept at applying the strategy, the materials with which they apply it can become more complex. As you proceed to more complex practice tasks, remember, however, that teacher-mediated practice should be given *before* having students independently use the strategy on these more difficult tasks. The nature of the materials, therefore, should be similar to that previously used when providing students with teacher-mediated practice activities.

Determining Mastery Levels of Strategy Performance

Earlier, when the strategy was practiced under teacher-mediated and peer-mediated conditions, mastery levels addressed two types of performance: (a) strategic functioning (the extent to which students correctly performed the strategy steps) and (b) performance outcomes (the results of using the strategy steps). At this point in the learning process, a third dimension of evaluation should be added: (c) *fluency*. Measures of fluency concern the extent to which students perform the strategy smoothly and independently; in some cases, they might also concern the speed with which the strategy is performed.

Measures of fluency are typically tied to measures of strategic functioning and performance outcomes. In other words, the strategy must be performed fluently but also lead to desired results (some students may be able to perform the strategy both fluently and independently but fail to produce any worthwhile results doing so). Indices of fluency typically address (a) the speed with which the strategy is performed and (b) the extent to which it is performed independently. For example, mastery levels of the Paraphrasing Strategy might consist of the following: "Given a 50-word paragraph, the student will, without assistance, paraphrase a correct main idea in less than 1 minute."

Unfortunately, measures of fluency do not easily address an important aspect of fluency—the degree to which the strategy is performed smoothly. Although it is possible to establish indices of fluency (e.g., combined speed and accuracy), your subjective judgment is often the most important factor in making decisions regarding whether students are smoothly performing the strategy. To make these subjective observations, you need to directly observe the student performing specific steps of the strategy. Be sure to watch for the transition between steps as well. If the student seems hesitant while performing some strategy steps or when transitioning, fluency has not been attained.

TIME CONSIDERATIONS

As a general guideline, students should demonstrate fluency for no less than 4 student-mediated applications of the strategy before proceeding to more difficult practice materials. Exercise caution, however, before proceeding to the next difficulty level. Students with learning disabilities (LD) often require several practices at mastery levels in order for fluency to become well established.

PROCEDURES

During the advanced organizer, inform students that they will be practicing independent use of the strategy at the current difficulty level in order to establish fluency. Your discussion might go something like this:

Up to this point, you have been practicing the new strategy in several different ways. We practiced it by you and me doing it together. You have also practiced it when working among yourselves as a team. Earlier, I was helping you a lot. Now you will be practicing the strategy by yourselves. Our goal is for you to be able to easily and smoothly apply the strategy—without help from others. In other words, now you will be learning to apply it independently and automatically.

This will be like when you learned how to ride a bike. When you first started practicing riding a bike, chances are you had training wheels to keep you from falling off. Then, when the training wheels were taken off, somebody probably ran beside you to help you control the bike and to keep you from crashing. Eventually, you had to take control of the bike and practice riding it without help until you were able to do it easily and automatically. When you first started practicing riding the bike without help, you had to really concentrate on all the things to do to keep from crashing. Eventually, however, you practiced it so much that now it's pretty much automatic. You just do it without worrying about how to do it. The major thinking that goes into riding a bike now is not so much how to ride it, but when and where you want to ride it and steering around obstacles that get in your way.

It's important for you to learn to use the strategy in a way similar to how you ride your bike. You need to learn to use it independently so that when you want to use the strategy to be more successful in your classes, or anywhere else you might use it, you'll be able to do so by yourself. You won't need me or anybody else. And when you come to an obstacle that makes the strategy hard to use, you'll know what to do to steer around it. You'll be independent and in charge of the situation.

You will continue practicing the strategy using materials at this difficulty level until you can perform it at mastery levels on four different occasions.

After providing students with a rationale for independent (self-mediated) practice, provide "advance feedback" based on past performance to individual students and have them set personal goals related to independent performance using the strategy. These goals should reflect both accuracy and fluency using the strategy.

Following students' independent practice attempts at using the strategy, you may wish to provide closure to the lesson by having them participate in a brief (e.g., 3- to 4-minute) group discussion regarding their experiences and perceptions while they were practicing. Below is an example of what you might say.

Well, you performed the strategy today pretty much by yourselves.
Did it seem hard or easy to you? Why?

What was the hardest part of the task? Why?

What was the easiest part? Why?

Did anybody run into any near snags or problems when using the strategy that you solved by yourself? What did you do? How did you know to do that?

How well did your solution to the snag work?

INSTRUCTIONAL DECISIONS

Once students have independently performed the strategy at mastery levels on four separate occasions, what should I do next? The answer to this question relates to the difficulty level of the materials a student has used. If the difficulty of the materials is very similar to that used in traditional classroom environments, then students are ready to begin learning how to create and use adaptations in the strategy to meet various setting demands. If the difficulty of the materials is still less difficult than those found in the regular class setting, then you should select materials that are more advanced than those previously used, and they should begin to approximate those found in the regular class environment.

Note: Remember that when students are advancing to the next difficulty level of materials, you may need to provide a limited degree of teacher-mediated practice and possibly some peer-mediated practice activities before students resume self-mediated practice activities.

TROUBLESHOOTING

What should I do if the student is not performing as well as anticipated? A guiding rule you can use in these circumstances concerns the degree to which the student is successful. If the student performs within 75% of the established mastery level, then the student should probably proceed with more independent practice. Goals for the next independent practice attempt should focus on specific areas of difficulty. Focused feedback should be provided. If, however, the student scores below 75% of the established mastery level, then you should consider providing more prompts and cues before moving on.

Advanced Practice

14

GOAL: To enable students to apply a strategy accurately and fluently to meet the demands of regular classroom settings.

ORIENTATION

Up to this point in the learning process, you have been providing students with instruction and practice activities designed to enable them to effectively perform the strategy under conditions that gradually approximated those found in regular classrooms. Eventually, students should be able to independently generalize the strategy to meet the demands they actually encounter in regular class settings. The advanced practice stage of instruction is an important turning point in the learning process; this stage is designed to bridge the gap between learning to perform the strategy and generalizing it for routine usage.

The advance practice stage of instruction is designed to assure that students take a proactive approach to regular classroom tasks by analyzing those tasks and discriminating when and how to use the strategy flexibly to meet their demands. To gain this level of competency, students practice applying the strategy to regular education tasks while still in a setting that can offer strategy support as needed (i.e., a support class). You may, at times, need to provide a degree of teacher mediation to help students decide how a strategy might be used in a given situation, but for the most part students should be mediating the process themselves. During this stage of instruction, teacher-directed feedback is rarely used.

Materials used during the advanced practice stage of instruction are either actual regular classroom assignments or tasks designed to closely approximate them. For example, providing advanced practice using the DEFENDS Writing Strategy might consist of having students apply the strategy in your support class setting to complete a homework assignment from their social studies class.

When there are no immediate opportunities to apply the strategy to regular class assignments, you will need to design some that closely simulate these. Guidelines for providing simulated real-life assignments are presented below:

Widely vary the nature of materials/activities that cue opportunities to use the strategy. Effective strategy users recognize when they are encountering opportunities to use a strategy. For example, they recognize specific questions on a study guide that call for the use of a paragraph writing strategy. During this stage of practice, you will need to vary the nature of cues that signal these opportunities. These cues should duplicate, as much as possible, the range of those that occur in the regular setting. For example, with the DEFENDS Writing Strategy you could provide students with opportunities to recognize cues signaling appropriate times to use the strategy, have students use the strategy to respond to practice essay test questions, current event reports, selected study guide questions from a social studies class, lab reports and selected end-of-the-chapter questions from a biology class, book reports from an English class, and so forth. If you were teaching the Paraphrasing Strategy, students would practice applying it to a host of reading materials they would likely encounter in school (e.g., textbooks, encyclopedias, magazine articles, newspapers).

Design tasks that require students to discriminate when to use the strategy as opposed to some other strategy. Students should be able to recognize when to use the strategy and when not to. To teach students to determine when to use an expository writing strategy, for example, you could provide them with a variety of writing tasks, for some of which use of an expository writing strategy is appropriate, some not. On one day you might require students to respond in writing to a prompt such as "Should President Nixon have been granted the 'executive privilege' of being immune from prosecution while in office?" This writing task simulates one that might typically be found in students' social studies classes; it would be appropriate to use an expository writing strategy in this situation because the question is asking the writer to take a position and defend it with reasons and supporting details. On another day you might ask students to respond in writing to the following: "Describe the parts of an amoeba"— a writing task that simulates those found on a biology lab worksheet. Use of an expository writing strategy would not be appropriate here because the query is strictly asking for a descriptive narrative (a strategy for writing descriptive paragraphs might be more appropriately used here).

Design tasks that will require students to practice using the strategy while interacting with poorly designed materials. Effective strategy users will make the best of a bad situation. Students, unfortunately, are often required to respond to instructional materials that are poorly designed. You should provide students with opportunities to become acclimated to using the strategy during these difficult circumstances so that they will be prepared for them in the future. For example, you might have students attempt to use the Paraphrasing Strategy when reading textbooks that are poorly written or use the DEFENDS Writing Strategy to compose a science report using poorly organized encyclopedia articles as information resources for the report.

PREPARATION

1. *Periodically meet with regular education teachers to identify specific upcoming tasks with which the strategy should be used.* Because the ideal form of advanced practice is applying the strategy to real-life assignments, you or the students will need to confer with their teachers to identify any upcoming assignments they will encounter in which the strategy can be applied. Be prepared to spend some time reviewing the various instructional materials students will encounter in these classes. You will need to review upcoming study guide questions, end-of-chapter questions, test questions, worksheets, and so forth (only a few, if any, questions on each may cue the use of the strategy). If possible, have the regular class teachers give you copies of the specific instructional materials with which the assignments will appear (e.g., study guides). You can show these to students later and ask them to look over the questions and decide which would be appropriate for applying the new strategy.

If students bring a regular class assignment in which use of the strategy is appropriate, and they express a desire to work on it in your support class setting, allow them to do so. In fact, you should strongly encourage students to recognize these opportunities and work on these types of assignments in your class. The advanced practice stage of instruction is the ideal time for this type of work.

2. *Periodically meet with regular class teachers to identify past tasks and assignments with which the strategy could have been used.* The second-best materials to use when providing advanced practice are actual tasks and assignments students have previously encountered in regular classroom situations. Once again you will need to study these to identify specific instances in which use of the strategy would have been appropriate.

Over time, you should attempt to build an extensive file containing copies of regular classroom assignments that can be used for advanced practice with different students. The assignments of every teacher in your school whom your students may encounter sooner or later should eventually be represented in this file. Similar regular class instructional materials can also be collected from other teachers and schools and used to help students learn to apply the strategy.[1]

3. *Design tasks and materials that closely simulate those encountered in regular classroom situations.* When designing tasks, be sure that they are represented by a wide variety of cues to use the strategy, that they present opportunities to practice discriminating between when to use the strategy and when not to, and that some provide opportunities for applying the strategy when interacting with poorly designed materials.

When designing these practice activities, modify existing instructional materials currently used in the regular classrooms if possible by integrating cues for strategy use. Look over all of the printed instructional materials used in the upcoming lesson (e.g., study guides, test questions, end-of-the-chapter questions) and analyze them to determine whether specific questions can be modified to include explicit cues to use the strategy. Rewrite the appropriate questions. The modified questions should provide subtle cues to use the strategy. For example, modifying the study guide question "List the three causes of the Civil War" to "Discuss three causes of the Civil War" provides students with an opportunity to (a) recognize an opportunity to use the DEFENDS Writing Strategy and (b) apply it, approximating interaction with the content currently

---

[1]If you know of other teachers who are providing instruction in the same strategy, you may find it very helpful to establish a network. This network can provide a forum for sharing materials gathered as well as those practice activities designed by you and other network teachers.

being addressed in the regular classroom.

By modifying existing regular class instructional materials, the advance practice activities in the support class setting will more closely approximate those that students will encounter in regular settings.

PROCEDURES

1. *Provide an advance organizer.* During the advance organizer, inform students that they will be practicing independent use of the strategy on tasks either taken from their regular classes or designed to simulate them. Note that the primary purpose of these practice activities is to ensure their using the strategy to effectively meet the demands of regular classrooms. Invite students to bring regular classroom assignments to which the strategy can be appropriately applied. Inform them that, for the most part, your role will be to monitor and you will assist them on a very limited basis.

2. *Have students utilize a proactive approach to the task.* Remember that effective strategy users not only perform the strategy with competence and confidence but also are proactive in their approach to the task. That is, they analyze the (materials and) task, determine how best to go about the task, and establish goals related to the task. At this point in the learning process, many students will proactively approach the task because of the way you have taught these skills in the past. Still, even at this late stage in the learning process, some students will impulsively plunge into the task without forethought. You may need to provide some structure for them, to assure they engage in a proactive approach to the task. A proactive approach can be structured by:

- *focusing students' attention on the stimulus materials.* Have them preview the materials to determine whether the strategy should or could be used. For example, to enable students' ability to discriminate when a paragraph writing strategy should be used when responding to end-of-chapter questions from a history class, have students look over all the questions and star those that they think should be answered using the strategy. Ask students to explain why they selected those particular questions.

- *focusing students' attention on goal setting.* Once students have previewed the assignment to determine opportunities to use the strategy, cue them to establish goals. Ask selected students to share their goals with you (these goals might reflect their concern for completing the assignment in a timely manner, performance outcomes related to using the strategy, attaining a desired grade, etc.).

3. *Have students perform the strategy.* Have students work on the advanced practice assignments. Provide cues and prompts only if the students really need them to perform the strategy.

4. *Provide opportunities for analysis of performance and feedback.* Of course, strategic learners analyze their performance in process. Reflection upon completing the task allows people to consider the "big picture" and to have hindsight. Once students have completed the assignment, encourage them to analyze their approach to the task and their work. Prompt them to reflect on what aspects of it reflect their best performance. Ask them to consider what was easy and difficult about the task as well as what they might do differently the next time they encounter a similar task.

After students have had an opportunity to reflect on their performance, have them share their observations with peers. This sharing time should be conducted in a reinforcing and encouraging manner so that the students are almost bragging about how they used the strategy to meet the regular classroom assignments. To facilitate the discussion, consider asking questions similar to the following:

> *When you were looking at the assignment, how did you know whether you should use the strategy or not?*
>
> *What was it about the study guide question [test question, etc.] that signaled you to use the strategy?*
>
> *What goals did you establish?*
>
> *Did you modify the strategy? How? How well did the modification work?*
>
> *Did it seem hard or easy to you? Why?*
>
> *What was the hardest part of the task? Why?*
>
> *What was the easiest part? Why?*
>
> *Did you run into any near snags or problems when using the strategy that you solved by yourself? What did you do? How did you know to do that? How well did your solution to the snag work?*
>
> *When you turn this in [or if you were to turn this in] to your regular classroom teacher, what grade do you think you'd get on it? What do you think the teacher would think about this work?*

*How does this work compare to what you would have done on this
task before you learned the strategy?*

During this time, it is important for students to learn how the strategy
was used by others to meet their various regular classroom tasks.

INSTRUCTIONAL DECISIONS

Determining mastery levels for advanced practice. Mastery levels of performance should be maintained at the same criteria as that established
when students were learning to use the strategy. At this point in the
learning process, however, you should introduce an additional mastery
criteria: *discrimination.* This measure concerns how well students make
decisions concerning when to use the strategy. For example, you may give
the students several assignments over a few days, only some of which
require the newly learned strategy. Observe the students' discrimination
in applying the strategy.

How much advanced practice is necessary? The amount of advanced
practice you provide students depends on the extent to which they, without help, (a) discriminate when to use the strategy and (b) perform the
strategy effectively when interacting with regular classroom assignments
or their equivalent. As a general guideline, students should complete a
minimum of four assignments at mastery levels before proceeding to the
next stage of instruction.

TROUBLESHOOTING

*What should I do if the student does not seem to be able to determine when
to use the strategy and when not to?* The most common difficulty students
encounter during advanced practice activities is discriminating when to
use the strategy. Most often, students who experience this difficulty need
practice making decisions as to when to use the strategy more than they
need practice applying the strategy. Be sure not to neglect actual strategy
practices, but plenty of "scrimmages" on deciding whether to use the
strategy should help.

Try designing activities in which the primary task is, for example, pre-
viewing instructional materials to select those questions or assignments

for which use of the strategy would be appropriate. Students should ana-lyze each question and decide whether the strategy should or should not be used, and tell why. If the strategy should be used, students should briefly tell how it would be used. Remember that the primary goal of this activity is to develop adeptness at making decisions regarding when to use the strategy. Students should not have to perform the strategy every time.

What should I do if the student is experiencing trouble applying the strategy on grade-level materials or tasks? There are several common reasons why students might experience difficulty performing the strategy on grade-level materials:

- *Students do not have sufficient content knowledge* to apply the strategy on advanced practice–level materials. Unfortunately, many students with mild learning problems do not accumulate a sufficient body of content knowledge to be able to effectively apply a new strategy. For example, if students have little or no knowledge of the dangers of having a one-crop agricultural economy, they will have very lim-ited success using a writing strategy when responding to a social studies assignment that requires them to answer the question, "How did cotton play a role in both the great economic success of the antebellum South and its demise?" Sometimes the problem associ-ated with the lack of content knowledge can be remedied, at least partially, by reviewing pertinent content information with students just prior to their performance of the strategy. Other times, students should not attempt to use the strategy because their lack of content knowledge is too great to overcome. For example, students should not attempt to paraphrase paragraphs from an auto mechanics text-book when they are very unfamiliar with a great deal of the termi-nology used in the chapter.

- *There was too big a leap in the difficulty of the task* between grade-level tasks in which they are currently attempting to apply the strategy and the difficulty level of previous practice activities. The best rem-edy for this problem is to design practice activities for which the difficulty gradually approximates grade level.

- *There was insufficient practice at easier levels.* Although students may have performed at mastery levels on easier-than-grade-level tasks, they may not have practiced the strategy enough on these easier tasks for it to become an ingrained approach. Try providing more practice at these easier levels before having them attempt to apply the strategy on grade-level materials.

- *Students are insufficiently motivated.* Although you may be tempted to use various extrinsic enticers to motivate students (e.g., extra credit, free time), you should not employ these unjudiciously. Perhaps more than any other stage in the learning process, the advanced practice stage marks the turning point in becoming independent strategy users. Overreliance on extrinsic reinforcements can reduce development of intrinsic reinforcement (motivation). There are many other dimensions to motivation you should also consider. For example, some students have become acclimated to a certain level of failure; they are used to it and have come to expect it. Other students may experience related, but different, motivation problems. Some may sense that learning to perform the strategy on grade-level tasks will, sooner or later, result in failure experiences. They may expend considerable energies maintaining a less successful level of performance in order to avoid the pain they fear will inevitably come if they attempt to perform on levels commensurate with their peers. To other students the cost–benefit ratio may become skewed. As students begin to apply the strategy on advanced practice materials, using the strategy may be too much trouble in relation to the relative benefits of doing so. For example, the comprehension a student gains as a result of using the Paraphrasing Strategy may simply be too little when compared to the amount of cognitive energy required to use it. These students may tend to use other, less taxing strategies, which they feel provide almost as much payoff as the more demanding strategies.

These are but a few of many complex reasons why students may be experiencing motivation problems at this stage of instruction. You will need to carefully analyze why students are experiencing these problems. One of the best things to do is to talk with individual students and find out what they say. During this discussion, describe different scenarios similar to those presented above and ask the students to tell which best describes what they are feeling. Some students are surprisingly honest about this subject.

Posttesting and Obtaining a Commitment To Generalize

GOAL: To confirm that the student has achieved mastery in learning the strategy and to establish the student's willingness to generalize the strategy to novel situations.

ORIENTATION

Even when a cook has served a marvelous meal, we say "the proof is in the pudding." The meaning of this saying can be interpreted in two ways. One way is that the job is not done well until it is done in its entirety. The other is that despite the success of any portion of the whole task, the final product (i.e., the pudding) is the most difficult and important measure. In the case of strategy instruction, we can paraphrase that old saying as "the proof is in the posttesting."

A posttest is a test that students take after concluding the advanced practice stage of strategy instruction. Unlike the success of the pudding (a British term for dessert), success on the posttest should be a fairly certain thing. A posttest is given to certify the students' achievement at learning the strategy. Throughout learning the strategy, the students have been charting their progress. As problems with learning the strategy were identified by you and the students, they were addressed. Each stage of instruction was not begun until the previous one had been successfully completed. Thus, students should not be considered ready for the posttest stage until they have successfully completed at least four advanced practice lessons. The posttest should not be too difficult for the student after this much successful practice at applying the strategy. The test, however, should be an honest and fair test. Once students have successfully passed the posttest, they should make a commitment to generalize the strategy to novel settings or tasks (just as a commitment to learn the strategy was made following the pretest).

PREPARATION

You are assessing the change in ability the student has achieved in completing a certain task. Thus, to make the most direct comparison to pretest performance possible, the posttest should approximate the pretest as closely as possible. When the student does not readily recall the pretest and correct responses to it (this is a form of *testwiseness*), it is appropriate to repeat it. Otherwise, develop a new test that is similar in such aspects as length and difficulty of individual items. Time considerations are the same as those for the pretest; allow the students to work uninhibited and unhurried. Also plan for time to review the test as soon as it is completed. Once posttest mastery has been achieved, time should also be scheduled to discuss strategy generalization with the students and obtain their commitment to generalize the strategy.

PROCEDURES

1. *Select an appropriate posttest.*
2. *Administer the posttest.*
3. *Evaluate the posttest with the student.*

(For each of these steps, refer back to the procedures for pretesting. Follow those same procedures for the posttest.)

4. *Discuss the importance of generalizing the strategy.* Remind the students that learning the strategy has been a means to an end. The purpose of learning a strategy is to improve both how they go about completing a task and their level of success. Stress that despite their success on the posttest, the students are not successful strategy users until they independently generalize strategy use to novel situations and tasks.

5. *Define* generalization *and discuss opportunities to generalize.* To generalize means to apply the strategy in ways and situations other than the practice activities used to learn it; be certain the students know this. To be certain they understand the concept of generalization, ask them to identify several areas in and out of school to which the newly learned strategy could be generalized. Bring along work samples from the students' regular education classes. Work with the students to identify when and how the strategy could be used to complete them. At this late stage in strategy learning, students should be doing the bulk of identifying when and how to use the strategy. Be sure to point out that in somè instances generalization of the strategy will mean slightly modifying how it is performed. For example, students should think about how they could use a modified version of the Paraphrasing strategy when watching a 40-minute film in science class. The modification might include note taking or making one general paraphrase with six or seven details to sum the entire film. You and the student should carefully evaluate which modifications are feasible and have fidelity to the strategy.

6. *Obtain the student's commitment to generalize use of the strategy.*

7. *Express a commitment to help the student generalize the strategy.*
(For these last two steps, refer back to and follow the corresponding steps from pretesting.)

PART III

Generalization

Orienting for Generalization

16

GOAL: To familiarize students with the concept of strategy generalization and to prepare them to generalize a newly learned strategy.

ORIENTATION

Generalization is a confusing concept. Some use the word *transfer* instead. Other's make a distinction between *transfer*—meaning to apply the strategy to novel tasks (e.g., using the Paragraph Writing Strategy for writing lesson summaries when it was used in practice only to respond to essay assignments)—and *generalization*—meaning to apply the strategy in novel ways (e.g., using the DEFENDS Writing Strategy to prepare a video project). Others think of generalization differently and refer to "near" and "far transfer" or generalization (Wong, 1994). From this perspective, the difference is in how much the current task resembles the type of task with which the strategy was learned.

To simplify the debate(s) on generalization, we can define it as the process of applying a strategy to novel situations and tasks. (Obviously, a rigorous discussion of the concept of generalization would not allow us to sidestep the important issues discussed above.) Despite the fact that most of us do not readily generalize the things we learn, generalization is far from impossible. When students are taught to generalize, they learn to do so. Research findings indicate that students of varied ability levels can and do learn to generalize SIM strategies when generalization is included as a phase of strategy teaching (e.g., Ellis, 1986; Ellis, Deshler, & Schumaker, 1989; Ellis, Lenz, & Sabornie, 1987a; Schmidt, Deshler, Schumaker, & Alley, 1989).

Generalization has been a persistent problem for strategy learning (regardless of whether SIM is used to teach strategies). Many students who have great success in learning how to perform a strategy fail to generalize its use. Reciprocally, many teachers who are excellent at teaching students how to perform a strategy fall short when teaching those students how to generalize the strategy. Generalization really is the whole point behind learning a strategy in the first place. Just as we often say that educated people are those who can think for themselves and think original ideas, strategic people are those who can perform a strategy independently (including determining when to use it) and make judicious decisions about how to apply it in novel situations. When students who successfully learn strategies, skills, or concepts fail to generalize them, we should say that they have not fully learned the strategy or skill; part of the fault must go to the teacher who did not complete the teaching task by effectively teaching the student to generalize.

PREPARATION

Preparation for this instructional activity is minimal. You should be sure that either you or the students bring along samples of the types of work from the students' regular education classes to which the strategy could be applied. You will also need to be sure that you are familiar with the concept of generalization so that you can discuss it with the students.

TIME CONSIDERATIONS

A single discussion session is all that is required to orient students for generalization.

PROCEDURES

1. *Review with the students the progress they have made to date in learning the strategy.* Using the students' progress charts, review how they have progressed from the pretest to the posttest in being able to perform the skills associated with the strategy. Have the students discuss the benefits of having learned the strategy thus far.

2. *Discuss generalization as the next phase of strategy learning.* First, define generalization. Although the students made a commitment to generalize following the posttest, they may not fully grasp the concept of generalization yet. Discuss precisely what it means to generalize a strategy, and provide lots of examples of generalization; remember to include examples of both types of generalization (or, generalization *and* transfer). To be certain the students understand the concept, ask them to generate several examples of generalization of the strategy, explaining why they are examples.

Second, discuss why generalization is an integral phase of strategy learning. Some students will consider their job done once they have passed the posttest and promised you they will generalize the strategy. Review the purposes for learning the strategy in the first place with the students (e.g., for students to be prepared to successfully complete tasks they will be given in regular classrooms when support teachers are not there to help them). Ask the students to explain why generalization is taught instead of everyone just trusting that the students will do it.

3. *Discuss when and how students can generalize the strategy.* Because you will be working together to ensure generalization is learned, you can use this opportunity to set generalization goals. Using materials from the students' classes, identify specific instances where they could generalize using the strategy. Discuss why these instances are appropriate. Be sure to also discuss exactly how the students would generalize the strategy in those specific contexts. The students can make lists of instances in which they could generalize the strategy and keep these lists handy (e.g., on the inside cover of a textbook or notebook) as ready reminders to generalize.

4. *Reconfirm the students' commitment to generalize.* Have the students affirm their commitment to generalize. This time include a statement of examples of where and how they may generalize the strategy.

Activating Generalization Through Plans and Assignments

GOAL: To facilitate students' use of a strategy across settings by providing assignments that require transfer of regular class tasks.

ORIENTATION

Generalization Assignments

During the activating generalization stage of instruction, you will provide students with two types of assignments: (a) teacher-directed transfer assignments and (b) student-initiated transfer assignments.

Teacher-Directed Transfer Assignments

Teacher-directed assignments require students to apply the strategy to tasks from another class. These assignments are completed using the strategy at home or in the regular classroom. Afterward, students meet with you to demonstrate and describe how the strategy was used to complete the assignment and to receive feedback.

The purpose of teacher-directed transfer assignments is to activate the generalization process by providing students with opportunities to build confidence in using the strategy independently and to become familiar with using it when support personnel (you) are not available.

When performing these teacher-directed assignments, responsibility for generalization is shared. You take the responsibility for recognizing the need to use the strategy and directing students' attention to this need; the students take responsibility for performing the strategy to meet the need. You and the students will share the responsibility for assessing how well the strategy was used to meet the regular classroom demands.

Student-Initiated Transfer Assignments

With student-initiated transfer assignments, the responsibility for generalization rests solely on students. In other words, students must recognize the need to use the strategy to meet a regular classroom demand and then use it independently at home or in regular classrooms. Afterward, students still meet with you to describe and demonstrate how the strategy was used, as well as to discuss the impact its use had in relation to meeting the regular classroom demands (e.g., how well the student was able to perform the task, how the regular teacher reacted to the student's use of the strategy, what grade was received on the work).

Setting Generalization Goals, Making Plans, and Monitoring

Facilitating generalization goal setting is a crucial component of the generalization process. Until this stage in the SIM, goals have focused on learning the strategy. Now students set goals related to recognizing opportunities for using the strategy and using it effectively and efficiently to successfully perform in criterion settings. Once these goals have been established, students create plans for operationalizing their goals and evaluating the effectiveness of these plans. Some techniques related to facilitating generalization goal setting are provided below.

Use Goal Sheets

You may find that generalization goal setting can be effectively facilitated using Generalization Goal Sheets, especially with strategies that produce permanent products (e.g., written paragraphs from a writing strategy, class notes from a notetaking strategy, study cards from a test-preparation strategy). A goal sheet simply provides a way of recording specific strategy use goals and progress toward meeting them. Its use also tends to provide the students and you documentation to spur appropriate followup. A goal sheet is easy to create. Some find it useful to write their goals directly on a progress chart such as that depicted in Figure 4.2.

Prior to generalizing the strategy, the students note the strategy to be used on the goal sheet, the regular class and setting demands for which it will be used, specific performance goals, a goal for a grade (if one is to be given), and dates indicating when the assignment is due and when which goals will be assessed. In addition, the students can note specific information about the assignment that is important to consider when performing the task.

After using the strategy to meet the specific setting demands, the students review with you the previously established goals and their performance of the strategy. The students indicate their grades earned, whether performance goals were met, and whether the assignment was completed and turned in on time. In addition, the students note specific strategic behaviors that they believe were performed best and those they need to try harder to use in the next generalization attempt.

Some teachers reject using goal sheets because of the paperwork involved. If you decide not to use the goal sheets, be sure that you cover the essential information addressed on the goal sheets when facilitating generalization goal setting with students.

Record Generalization Progress

If students charted their progress to mastery as they learned the new strategy, you probably noticed how motivating this activity was for them. You will likely find that students' charting their progress toward generalization is equally effective.

A line graph is a useful way of charting progress. To construct one, plot the date or name of each generalization across the bottom (x axis), and along the side (y axis) list the point scale with the lowest score at the bottom (e.g., 0 to 100). For each generalization, place a dot at the score earned, and connect the dots as you (the student) go. (Of course, other forms of appropriate charts or graphs that you and the student prefer are equally acceptable.) These charts are particularly useful for those strategies with which use results in permanent products that are subsequently scored (e.g., using a paragraph-writing strategy produces written work; class notes provide evidence of using a note-taking strategy).

Make Students' Generalization Goals Public

When students make their goals public, they are more likely to attain them (see Adelman & Taylor, 1983; Ellis, 1986; Ellis, Lenz, & Sabornie, 1987a, 1987b). These are several ways to facilitate making goals public:

- Have each student review her or his performance goals with another student.

- Arrange to have students complete individual Generalization Goal Sheets when interacting in a group format. Students work together to establish individual goals.

- Make public group goals. For example, one teacher teaching the DEFENDS Writing Strategy posted the following sign outside of her classroom door:

> Last week, 6 out of 8 students used DEFENDS at mastery levels in social studies, history, and English classes. The average grade on our writing assignment was B+.
>
> This week, our goal is to have 7 out of 8 students use DEFENDS at mastery levels in these classes. Our goal for an average grade is A−.

Another teacher posted the following sign on her door:

> This is the fourth week in a row in which at least 6 of our students received an A on a writing assignment using DEFENDS.
>
> Our goal for this week is:
>
> - make it five weeks in a row
>
> - show an average of 10% improvement over last week's use of DEFENDS.

- Publicly post individual or group performance charts, if both the students who do and do not get theirs posted are comfortable with this. For some students, posting goals but not outcomes may be a more acceptable incentive. Have students plot points on the chart that indicate their goals for the next generalization attempt, and then later plot actually attained scores. For example, if a student sets a goal of .10 mechanical errors for writing, this goal is plotted on the chart. Then the student's actual mechanical writing score on the generalization attempt is plotted for comparison.

Specify Assignments Anticipated in Regular Class Setting To Facilitate the Establishment of Performance Goals for These Assignments

Many students will need help initially in structuring generalization goals. You can provide this assistance by meeting with them at the beginning of the school day or week and asking them to think about their various classes to anticipate tasks they will probably encounter, with which the strategy could be used. After you have worked with your students to identify these opportunities, they will establish specific goals for applying the strategy, and when appropriate, set performance goals as well.

Facilitate the Setting of Daily and/or Weekly Goals That Focus on Students Recognizing Opportunities To Use the New Strategy As Well As Establishing Performance Goals for These Assignments

Here, responsibilities for generalizing the strategy are placed more squarely on students. In earlier stages of instruction, you were informing students about upcoming regular classroom assignments and facilitating goal setting with regard to these assignments. The emphasis shifts now so that students also take responsibility for recognizing opportunities to use the new strategy and establish performance goals. To facilitate this form of goal setting, you should first review with the students potential opportunities for using the strategy as well as cues to use the strategy that may be forthcoming in each of the students' classes. Then students set goals regarding using the strategy, following which they set performance goals regarding its use.

Reinforcing Generalization of the Strategy

Make Generalization a Prestigious Act

Because independent generalization of the strategy represents the pinnacle of mastering the procedure, these events should be recognized accordingly. Many teachers have found it useful to establish "Generalization Clubs." Students are eligible to join this club when they have demonstrated successful generalization a set number of times (you and your students should decide how many generalizations should be required). Members' names are posted publicly on a plaque or chart. When a student is initiated into the club, it should be somewhat of a formal procedure. Key persons (e.g., former members of the Generalization Club, principal, parents or guardians, significant regular teachers, as well as other students who are learning the strategies) can be invited for refreshments to celebrate the students' initiation.

The Generalization Club serves two purposes. First, it is reinforcing to become a member. Second, it serves as a motivator to students who are just beginning to learn the strategy. When students see the names of friends and upperclass students who are members, they realize that others, just like themselves, have mastered the strategy and *used* it to be more successful in their regular classes.

Incorporate Use of Formal Student Generalization Reports

Although students will be reporting to you regarding their use of the strategy, requiring students to make formal presentations to their peers regarding their experiences generalizing the strategy can be an effective way of reinforcing their effective usage. Students can be assigned a specific day when the presentation is due. During the report, the student tells her or his peers about a specific regular classroom assignment for which the strategy was used, discusses how the strategy was used, shares copies of permanent products that resulted from using the strategy, and shares with peers what happened as a result of using the strategy (e.g., grades, comments, compliments).

Publicly Post Permanent Products That Reflect Use of the Strategy

If use of the strategy results in a permanent product that shows evidence that the strategy was used, these products can be publicly posted in the classroom. For example, you might wish to post in your classroom any regular classroom papers that reflect students' use of the DEFENDS Writing Strategy. Each time students bring you a paper that reflects use of the strategy, the paper is taped next to the previous one. Eventually, a chain of papers reflecting use of the strategy will begin to wrap around the walls of your room. The longer the chain, the more motivated students are to bring you additional papers that reflect generalization.

IMPLEMENTING TEACHER-DIRECTED TRANSFER ASSIGNMENTS

To assure that students begin using the strategy in regular classroom settings, you will be giving students specific assignments that require them to transfer use of the strategy to other settings. Students will report back to you for feedback and to discuss how it was used. Students will record performance scores on generalization progress charts.

Preparation

1. *Plan teacher-directed activation assignments.* You should plan on assigning students at least six different transfer assignments. These assignments must be completed in settings other than the support class setting. These assignments can either simulate those found in a regular classroom situation (e.g., require students to use the DEFENDS Writing Strategy to write a current events report even though such a report is not due for social studies class) or duplicate specific assignments in a regular class (i.e., the same product can be used to complete an actual class assignment). If you plan to give assignments that duplicate those in regular class settings, you will need to meet with regular class teachers to identify the upcoming assignments with which the strategy can be applied.

2. *Prepare generalization progress charts.* The progress charts used to indicate performance on transfer tasks can be very similar to those used earlier when students were practicing the strategy during the advanced practice state of instruction. Students should be able to plot accuracy scores for each practice attempt—the key difference being that the strategy was not performed in the support class setting. For each practice attempt, the chart could have space to indicate where the strategy was performed.

Time Considerations

You should allow adequate time for students to complete each teacher-directed transfer assignment (remember, they have other assignments and obligations) and then meet to debrief (e.g., discuss how the strategy was used, review goals and plans as necessary, and record progress).

Procedures

1. *During the advance organizer, provide a rationale for teacher-directed assignments.* Inform students that they will be practicing using the strategy in settings other than the one in which the strategy was learned so that they can become confident in using it independently.

2. *Provide students with transfer assignments.* Direct students to complete the specific transfer assignment, and make sure they understand what they are expected to do. Provide a specific due date for completing the assignment and make appointments with students for debriefings.

3. *After they have finished transfer assignments, debrief students and mediate assessment procedures.* Meet with students to discuss how the strategy was used. Provide cues, as necessary, to prompt students to self-evaluate their performance. The following are potential areas to consider when discussing use of the strategy and evaluating performance:

- How well the strategy was performed

- How much help was needed

- How current levels of performance on the transfer task would translate into measures of success in the regular classroom

- What characteristics of the setting in which the strategy was used made the strategy easier or more difficult to perform

- What aspects of the task made it difficult to perform the strategy

- What aspects of the strategy students most successfully performed

- What aspects of the strategy were most difficult to perform

- What aspects of the strategy students need to focus more energies on performing effectively on future transfer tasks, as well as how they plan to perform these aspects more effectively

- How close students' performances came to meeting their goals

- How well students used self-motivation procedures

- What students did to remember to complete the transfer task

2. *Have students record their generalization progress.* Have them record their performance on a generalization progress chart.

Instructional Decisions

Is it appropriate to begin teaching another strategy even though students have not completed this phase of instruction? Since the major portion of your instruction in the strategy has been completed, beginning to teach a new strategy is appropriate at this time. Students often think that they are "finished" with the strategy they have been learning. Thus, they should be informed that they are simply entering a new phase of instruction on the strategy. The current phase allows for overlap so that they will be learning two things: how to transfer the strategy recently mastered and how to use a new strategy.

Troubleshooting

If students need to be weaned from your support and the shelter provided by the support class setting: Occasionally some students will experience difficulty with the teacher-directed assignments because they lack confidence in themselves and have grown dependent on you and your classroom for support, or it is truly a novel form of schooling for them. You may need to structure transfer assignments. For example, you may need to specify the setting in which the student is to perform the strategy; say something such as:

> *Here's a hall pass. Please go to the library and use the Paraphrasing Strategy as you read a magazine article. After you've finished, come back and we'll talk about it.*

For very dependent students, you may facilitate completion of teacher-directed assignments by gradually increasing the distance between the support setting and the setting in which the students are to complete the transfer assignment. For example, the student might complete the assignment in the empty classroom next door, next time in a study hall, and so on.

IMPLEMENTING STUDENT-INITIATED TRANSFER ASSIGNMENTS

Preparation

Prepare Generalization Club charts. If you choose to use the "Generalization Club" as a means for motivating students, you should create progress charts so that they can be shared with the students. Design your own, or have students design and create them.

Prepare Generalization Goal Setting Sheets. In designing a generalization goal setting sheet, remember that critical elements to include are places for the student to indicate the regular class and assignment for which the strategy was used as well as a place to note what happened as a result of using the strategy.

Time Considerations

Students should successfully perform at least four student-initiated transfer assignments. The amount of time required to complete this phase of instruction, therefore, will depend on the frequency with which students have opportunities to use the strategy in regular classroom situations.

Procedures

1. *During the advance organizer, provide a rationale for student-initiated assignments.*

2. *Provide students with timelines for transferring use of the strategy.* You should be somewhat familiar with how often the student will have opportunities to use the strategy to meet regular classroom demands. Use this information to establish a timeline regarding when the results of student-initiated transfer assignments are expected. Direct students to complete the specific transfer assignment, and make sure they understand what they are expected to do. Provide a specific due date for completing the assignment and make appointments with students for regular debriefings.

3. *Establish due dates for formal student generalization reports.* The frequency with which generalization reports are provided in your classroom will naturally depend on how many students are learning the strategy and what else is going on. Ideally, at least one generalization report will be made by one of your students each week. Thus, a single student might give only one generalization report a month.

4. *After they have finished transfer assignments, debrief students and mediate assessment procedures.* When debriefing students' self-initiated use of the strategy to meet a regular classroom demand, you will be discussing the same points as those discussed when debriefing on the results of teacher-directed assignments. In addition, you might wish to discuss with the students how they recognized the opportunity to use the strategy and the results of using it.

5. *Have students record their student-initiated generalization progress.* Have students record their performance on a generalization progress chart.

6. *Have students present to others their experiences generalizing the strategy in formal presentations.* One way to structure the student generalization report is to have the student use the generalization goal setting sheet as a set of notes. Ask the student to:

- Name the strategy
- Briefly describe the strategy steps
- Tell for what class and assignments the strategy was used
- Describe the critical features or key aspects of the assignment that were important to consider for success
- Describe the cues that signaled the student that it was a good time to use the strategy
- Tell what goals the student established before using the strategy
- Describe how the strategy was used
- Show and/or describe results of using the strategy
- Tell what aspects of performing the strategy are the student's best work
- Tell what aspects of the strategy the student intends to work harder at correctly using in the future

- Discuss what other opportunities there have been to use the strategy, and what happened

7. *Encourage students' peers to reinforce the students' attempts at generalizing the strategy, and facilitate student dialogue about generalization experiences.* You can cue other students to discuss use of the strategy as well as reinforce the student giving the report by asking them to:

- Tell what part of the student's work they think was best

- Relate their own experiences to the student's

- Tell how they used the strategy in similar circumstances

- Tell what they learned from the student that they can use when they are generalizing the strategy

Instructional Decisions

Can teacher-directed transfer assignments and student-initiated transfer assignments overlap? In most cases, these generalization techniques can be implemented simultaneously. Some students, however, may require practice with more structured transfer tasks provided by the teacher-directed assignments before they are ready to self-initiate transfer.

Troubleshooting

Sooner or later you will encounter students who seem to respond well to the teacher-directed assignments but do not initiate use of the strategy independently. If students do not seem motivated to independently use the strategy, then you may wish to use extrinsic reinforcers. Chances are, however, the students are not transferring use of the strategy because they are not recognizing opportunities to use it. Peers and/or regular class teachers can be enlisted to cue strategy use. Procedures for using peers to cue students are described below. Procedures for using regular classroom teachers to promote strategy use are described in the section that follows.

Use peer facilitators. Have students cue each other to use the strategy. To implement such a process, consider the following steps:

- Identify all of your students (from your entire roll, not just those from a specific class/group) who are learning the strategy who also are assigned a specific regular class teacher.

- Determine which of these students attend the same regular class at the same time. Pair students who attend the same regular classes at the same time.

- Meet with each pair of students and discuss the need to cue each other to use the strategy in the specific regular classroom. Establish goals for cueing each other.

- Meet with the regular class teacher and explain the purpose of using peer facilitators. Discuss how you hope to arrange for the students to cue each other to use the strategy in order to promote generalization. Arrange to have students sit close to each other to facilitate cueing.

Use regular class teachers as facilitators. Here are some helpful ideas:

- Share the purpose of the strategy and the student's success to date when using it.

- Teach the teachers cues to strategy use they can incorporate into their teaching and signs they can watch for that the student is using it.

- Check-in with teachers regarding the student's strategy use processes and progress.

Adapting Generalization

18

GOAL: To help the student learn how to apply part or all of the strategy in novel ways.

ORIENTATION

So far in the generalization phase of SIM instruction, the student has participated in becoming "oriented" to the concept of generalization and practicing activating generalization by being able to determine when and where to apply the strategy. The next aspect of generalization is what some refer to as *far transfer*. Students extrapolate parts of the overall strategy, sometimes slightly modifying them, to use them with novel tasks. That is to say, they will be adapting the strategy to meet demands for which the strategy would not be readily useful in its original form.

Adaptive generalization will not come automatically to students simply because they have become proficient at activating generalization. Activation is, however, a prerequisite to adaptation for most students. While there may be some overlap in teaching activation and adaptation, students should be fairly proficient at identifying situations appropriate for the strategy before they attempt to determine how to extrapolate and alter parts of the strategy to complete novel tasks.

An example may make this point more clear. Say that a student has been assigned to read Robert Frost's and Maya Angelou's presidential inaugural poems and to identify the major themes each poet has expressed; once having done this, the student is to report the major themes of each by making a collage of photographs. A student who is proficient at identifying when the Paraphrasing Strategy may be helpful would recognize that this task is not quite like those learned with the Paraphrasing Strategy but is similar to them. Another student who is just beginning to identify appropriate tasks independently would probably not see the similarity and be able to make the adaptation decisions that follow. The student who is proficient at adaptation, however, could recognize that she or he could chunk sections of each poem (perhaps by stanzas) and ask her- or himself questions such as "What is the topic (theme) the author is presenting in this chunk?" and "What evidence do I have that that is a theme?" In this case, the student has recognized that self-questioning is involved in the strategy and that questions are asked specifically about the nature of the information sought (i.e., themes vs. main ideas and details). In addition, the student has understood the logic of breaking at paragraphs and generalized this to the structure of the two poems. These are advanced tasks that students can do with some initial guidance but that cannot be reasonably expected of them on their own. This is not an aspersion on students; rather, we are all unlikely to make adaptive generalizations until we have gained some prerequisite knowledge.

PREPARATION

Materials you will need for this lesson are minimal. They include sample assignments from the students' classes for which the strategy can be adapted. If you can put your hands on recent samples of when the student tried to apply the strategy but it turned out to be inappropriate, bring these too. Visiting with the students' teachers to discuss the nature of tasks done in their classes will also be helpful.

TIME CONSIDERATIONS

A single meeting should be held with the student to present the concept of adaptive generalization. Allow enough time to review this concept and to model examples of adapting the new strategy. Once the student begins to adapt the strategy, you should phase out your participation in the process of identifying appropriate situations and specifying adaptations.

PROCEDURES

1. *Discuss the concept of adapting generalization.* Begin by reviewing the general definition of generalization and the definition of activating generalization. Ask the student to identify the limits of this type of generalization. If the student does not identify that the strategy is limited to tasks quite similar to those with which it was learned, you should make this point.

Define and provide examples of adaptive generalization. These examples should be simple adaptations. To check understanding ask the student to identify examples of strategy adaptation. If the student cannot do this yet, ask for examples from everyday life. For example, you could ask the stumped student to explain how chewing gum could be used to temporarily stop a tent leak.

2. *Discuss what goes into adaptive generalization.* Identify that a strategy is a series of substrategies. For example, in the Paraphrasing Strategy, the student (a) begins by reading, (b) asks the self questions, (c) searches for cues to answer the questions, (d) transforms the information and expresses the transformed information. In fact, there are even more substrategies involved (e.g., making decisions about accepting or rejecting individual units of content as answers to the questions, determining that the transformed information is personally comprehensible and true to the original concept found in the paragraph), but these major substrategies are what will be adapted. The substrategies of any strategy can be identified by thoughtfully listing all of the overt and cognitive activities committed with each step of the strategy. Similarly, the student should practice identifying the subtasks of an assignment. For example, in the inaugural poems assignment, the student needs to (a) read a poem, (b) determine where to break the poem into the equivalent of paragraphs (or based on some other unit) and ask the self questions, (c) search for cues, and (d) transform the information and express it in collage form.

3. *Identify instances of when the strategy could be adapted as well as how.* Using materials from the students' classes and other materials on which their practice attempts have failed, practice identifying strategy adaptations. Initially you should model and describe how you would make the adaptations. Gradually involve the students in the modeling and descriptions. After several of these examples, ask the students to generate examples on their own. You should be sure to constructively critique these examples with the individual students.

4. *Practice adaptive generalizations.* Under your guidance initially students should practice adapting the strategy on actual school tasks. Gradually turn responsibility over to the students for adapting the strategy. Have the students keep a record of when and how they adapted the strategy as well as of how their adaptations worked.

Generalization Maintenance

19

GOAL: To ensure that the student continues to use a newly learned strategy and has success using it correctly.

ORIENTATION

By the time students have become accomplished at adaptive generalizations of the strategy, they should be regarded as independent strategic learners. Just like all of us, however, they will need occasional checks to make certain the strategy is being used correctly and with success. Think of the old adage about something well learned being "like riding a bicycle—once you learn, you never forget." This may be so, but someone who has not ridden a bicycle in several years would be wise to wear a helmet the first few times back on one. The same principle is true for strategy users. If for some reason students have no cause to use the strategy for a while, they may not think about using it when the opportunity finally arises again. Also, bad habits such as shortcuts in procedures tend to creep into one's repertoire. In short, there are many reasons why students who have learned and practiced a strategy and even shown great proficiency at generalizing it would fall into a rut of using it incorrectly or stop using it all together.

Periodic maintenance checks can be used to determine whether the student is (a) using the strategy when appropriate, (b) using the strategy correctly, and (c) having success as a result of using the strategy. (Of course, "using" here means both applying the strategy as it has been learned *and* activation and adaptive generalization.) These checks do not have to be time consuming. Part of the responsibility for them can be turned over to the students. Students should have an intrinsic motivation to continue using the strategy. These checks can serve to bolster that motivation by signaling to the students that you and other teachers continue to expect them to use it. The checks also serve to signal you as to when you need to do some troubleshooting with students if they are having problems using the strategy. Unfortunately, in the busy routines of schools, simple problems such as confusing how to apply a strategy tend to go unnoticed until they become major problems for students. Thus, when necessary, generalization maintenance means reviewing strategy procedures with the student.

PREPARATION

As with the other generalization lessons, preparation for generalization maintenance checks is minimal. Sample materials such as those with which the students have done advanced practice should be used. Also have on hand charts and records of the students' progress in learning the strategy and copies of any cue cards the students have used in the past.

TIME CONSIDERATIONS

Allow enough time for the students to discuss with you their experiences in using the strategy. Following this discussion the students will do a practice activity that you will score in the same way that pretest, practice lesson, and posttest activities were scored. Schedule enough time for the students to do this activity and participate in scoring and discussing the results. In the event some students do not do well on the maintenance check, time will also have to be scheduled when you can review and practice the strategy together.

PROCEDURES

There are two stages to generalization maintenance. First, a generalization progress check is made. This includes a quick review of strategy use and a maintenance probe (actually a test) of the students' strategy performance. Second, strategy reviews or future maintenance checks are planned, based on outcomes of the maintenance probe.

Check on Progress

1. *Review the students' experiences in using the strategy.* Help to set the tone for the maintenance check to be a supportive experience as opposed to an adversarial one by asking students to discuss what has gone right in using the strategy. For example, ask students to identify instances when they have used the strategy. Probe for information on how the strategy was used and the results the students attribute to using the strategy. Also ask whether other teachers have supported the students' using the strategy by doing such things as cueing its use and not insisting that students follow procedures that prohibit strategy use. You may discover that some of the students' teachers would benefit from a "maintenance check" in which you review with them the importance of the students' using the strategy. In this portion of the conversation you should also ask students to identify any problems with strategy use that they have noticed. Be sure to recognize the students positively for identifying any such problems on their own. If the problems are minor (e.g., running out of copies of the organizer form used with the DEFENDS Writing Strategy, or having difficulty composing mnemonic device words for the FIRST-Letter Mnemonic Strategy), discuss strategies for overcoming them (e.g., using scrap paper for organizer forms, or inserting letters to create words).

2. *Review the steps and procedures for using the strategy.* As a check of the students' recall of the strategy steps and procedures, ask them to name the steps of the strategy and explain what actions are taken with each step. Be sure that the students discuss both the overt and cognitive activities of each step. If students have trouble articulating how a step is performed, ask them to describe an example of performing that step. You can then work together to describe the overt and cognitive activities involved. When students cannot describe the actions, they are signaling that their grasp of them is tenuous. You can then work together to "dissect" specific examples. Because students generate the examples, they should be able to articulate how they are performed. You can coach their descriptions with leading questions. Once the student has described how the step is performed, discuss what the overt and cognitive activities are. Be sure that in these discussions you do not limit yourself to talking about how the strategy is conventionally performed. Also discuss ways to generalize the strategy and the processes that go into activation and adaptive generalizations.

3. *Assess the students' current strategy performance.* Explain to the students that they will be taking a "test" of how well they perform the strategy. The test will be similar to the pretest and posttest. Stress that this is a checkup and not an attempt to be punitive. An analogy such as a dental checkup or an automobile tune-up may be helpful. The student could generate scenarios of why those checkups are done and what types of outcomes are possible (e.g., come back in 6 months, get a filling right away). Have the student complete the maintenance test independently and free of interruptions and distractions.

4. *Score the test and review the results with the students.* To make the feedback most meaningful, score the test immediately upon the students' completion of it. Have the students go over the scoring with you. You may point out particular strengths and weaknesses in their performance and ask them to explain them. In the case of errors, always ask the students how the errors could be corrected and how those same types of errors can be avoided in the future. Tabulate a total score for each student and compare it to the mastery level the student used all throughout learning the strategy. Posting this maintenance score on the student's progress chart is a good idea.

Determine Where To Go Next

Based on how well each student did on the maintenance test, the two of you will select one of two options: review and practice specific aspects of the strategy and then retest for mastery, or proceed directly to scheduling the next maintenance check.

1. *Review and practice specific aspects of the strategy.* If some students do not achieve mastery on the maintenance test, determine specifically what aspects of performing the strategy were problematic for them. Schedule sessions in which you can review the strategy process and the students can engage in advance practice activities. Continue the advance practice activities until the students have attained mastery on at least four practice attempts. (Do not begin with these practice attempts;" rather, first spend time together reviewing and practicing strategy performance.) Once again, ask the students to take a posttest to validate that they have again mastered the strategy. Once mastery is again achieved, discuss with the students how they can avoid experiencing the same slip in performance in the future.

2. *Schedule future maintenance checks.* Remind the students of the purpose of maintenance checks. They should not feel that they are punitive actions but rather a common part of keeping their strategicness "tuned up." Decide together how long to wait before having another maintenance check. You can, of course, schedule periodic times to simply talk about how strategy use is going. Also discuss whether there are potential problems with a particular teacher or task. You may want to be sure that you both monitor these situations so that a problem can be promptly addressed should it come up. Be sure to leave students on a positive note. They have reached quite a milestone to have come this far in the learning process.

PART IV

Strategies in
Inclusive Classrooms

Regular Class Teachers Cooperating To Support Strategy Use

GOAL: To work with regular education teachers to ensure instruction that promotes strategy generalization.

ORIENTATION

While the bulk of responsibility for generalization of a new strategy lies with the student, the regular class teacher can do several things to promote transfer of the strategy. Her or his providing the student with cues and prompts to use the strategy when appropriate can have a significant impact on the degree to which the student generalizes strategy use. You and the regular education teacher should routinely communicate about how well the student is meeting the demands the strategy is designed to satisfy. Specific techniques focus on supportive teaching procedures and integration of cues to use the strategy into daily teaching and materials.

Supportive Teaching Procedures

Although content-area teachers are primarily responsible for teaching their subject matter, there are some relatively simple things they can do to help the generalization process. These include cueing, prompting, modeling, and reinforcing.

Cue Use of the Strategy

You will probably find that many of your students who have mastered the strategy subsequently fail to use it in regular classroom situations. Fortunately, a simple reminder, or cue, to use the strategy usually results in its efficient use. Quick cues provided by regular education teachers can be very beneficial. For example:

> This is a good time to use the Paraphrasing Strategy.

Three ways to provide these simple cues are to (a) discretely tell a specific student to use the strategy, (b) ask the entire class to use the strategy, and (c) have those who know the strategy prompt their peers who may be forgetting to use it.

Prompt Use of the Strategy

Some students who do not seem to respond to cues to use the strategy may have forgotten parts of it. In these cases, the regular education teacher can prompt the student to perform specific aspects of the strategy. For example, the teacher can ask the student to say or list the steps of the strategy and to explain how to perform them. For example,

> This is a good time to do the DEFENDS Writing Strategy. Varda, help me remember the steps. What does the D step tell me to do?

Model the Strategy

There may be situations in which the strategy can be applied to a regular classroom task, but the student is not sure *how* to apply it to that task. For example, although students may be adept at paraphrasing when reading textbook passages, they may not know how to use the strategy to interpret visual aides in the textbook. Here, the regular class teacher might model how to paraphrase the main idea depicted in the visual as well as how to make decisions when selecting the most pertinent details in the visual. After modeling use of the strategy, the teacher should then prompt students to try the strategy with this novel application.

Provide Reinforcement and Feedback to Students for Using the Strategy

Perhaps one of the most powerful techniques for facilitating generalization of the strategy is for persons in the same setting (e.g., the regular classroom teacher, support staff working in the regular classroom) to recognize students for using the strategy. Examples of brief reinforcing comments that can be very effective are provided below:

> I noticed you were using the Paraphrasing Strategy when we were going over those paragraphs today. Good choice.
> When you answered the essay question on the test, it looked like you were using DEFENDS. That was a smart thing to do.

The teacher can promote generalization by cueing students to reinforce themselves in the form of self-congratulatory statements. For example:

> I noticed you were using the Paraphrasing Strategy when we were going over those paragraphs today. You should congratulate yourself for recognizing a good time to use the strategy.
> When you answered the essay question on the test, it looked like you were using DEFENDS. What should you tell yourself when you do a smart thing like that?

Another way to reinforce students for generalizing the strategy is by providing extrinsic rewards such as extra credit or bonus points for using the strategy to meet a regular classroom demand.

Still another form of reinforcement, no less effective, is to have the teacher ask the student who has learned the strategy to either tell the entire class about the strategy and how it can be used to perform better on tasks or teach the strategy to another student in the class.

Providing feedback concerning students' use of the strategy appears to be an important facilitator of generalization. The regular class teacher might take a few moments to provide the student with explicit feedback concerning how well the student did or did not use the strategy in a specific instance or when the student failed to recognize opportunities to use the strategy.

Modifying Daily Instruction and Materials and Communicating the Expectation of Strategy Use

The regular class teacher can promote generalization of the strategy by integrating cues to use the strategy into daily instruction. By integrating these cues, a message is communicated to students that there is an expectation that the strategy will be used.

Working Relationships Between Support Teachers and Regular Education Teachers

Because regular class teachers can play a significant role in the students' generalization of the strategy, you should communicate with them about the strategy and the students who are learning, or have learned, the strategy.

Meet with Regular Education Teachers To Assess Setting Demands Before Teaching the Strategy

Before teaching a strategy to students, you should have met with their teachers to assess the regular class setting demands to help you decide which strategy students should learn. There should be a clear match between what the strategy is designed to accomplish and what students are expected to do to be successful in their regular classes.

Meet with Regular Education Teachers Periodically As the Student Is Learning the Strategy

During the period in which students are learning the strategy, regular education teachers should be kept informed of the students' progress toward mastery. There are several reasons why this is important. It reiterates the role of the support teacher as being the instructor of strategies (as opposed to a glorified tutor). It also serves to confirm the important setting demands. Regular education teachers are in a position to know what to expect from your students (these expectations often must be raised). It also serves as a way to educate regular education teachers about the specific strategy the student is learning and how, by learning this strategy, the student will be in a better position to succeed in the regular class (in turn, making the job of the regular class teacher easier). Also, regular education teachers learn how they can facilitate generalization by using supportive procedures and integrating cues into routine instruction and materials.

Meet with Regular Teachers Periodically After the Student Has Mastered the Strategy

Once students have mastered the strategy and begun the activating generalization stage of instruction, you should continue to periodically meet with their regular education teachers to (a) enlist their assistance to help students solve problems related to applying the strategy and (b) assess whether the student is appropriately generalizing the strategy.

INITIATING REGULAR EDUCATION TEACHERS' USE OF SUPPORTIVE TEACHING PROCEDURES

The purpose of supportive teaching is to enlist assistance from students' regular education teachers to facilitate generalization of the strategy. Regular education teachers will be modifying their instructional style and materials to facilitate use of the strategy in regular classroom settings. Specific suggestions for implementing supportive teaching are provided below.

Preparation

Finding a Meeting Time That Is Mutually Convenient

One of the key ingredients to successful working relationships is finding a meeting time that is acceptable to all participants. There are two approaches you can take. One is to plan on meeting with individual teachers separately. An advantage of this approach is that you are able to focus attention on the specific students who attend a teacher's class. A disadvantage is that you must arrange to meet individually with each different regular education teacher. You will find yourself trying to schedule meetings during lunch, planning periods, after school, and so on; as a result, you will have little time for your own instructional planning and mental health. Alternatively, try to meet with them as a group (probably either before or after school). Advantages of meeting with teachers as a group is that you are able to communicate the same message once (e.g., what the strategy is, how it is designed to help students meet their regular class demands, how they can help facilitate generalization via supportive teaching). Another advantage is that you may find teachers more willing to support strategies when they see other teachers participating. In this way, responsibility for supporting strategy use becomes shared. You may find that the teachers' perspectives gradually shift from viewing the situation as the students' problem and *your* job to "fix it" to one of shared responsibility for dealing with it. This can mean accepting that the "problem" is with how the student is taught and not within the student. This is not always easy for teachers to accept. The major disadvantage to this approach is having teachers participate in "another meeting."

Preparing Materials for the Regular Education Teachers

Since you will be asking regular class teachers to participate in strategy teaching activities (e.g., cueing, prompting, modeling), they will need specific information that will allow them to understand what to do and how to implement those procedures with minimal effort. Teachers should be provided with two items. First, provide them with a copy of the strategy steps, taking time to explain them. Second, provide them with written information on how they can encourage students' strategy use. For example, you could list situations when the teacher could cue students to use the strategy (e.g., verbally cue students to use DEFENDS when answering a study guide question) as well as how the teacher might reinforce its use (e.g., give bonus points to students who turn in a completed organizer form). You can brainstorm with the teacher to list additional instances when students could be cued to use the strategy.

Time Considerations

Meet with teachers (either individually or as a group) a minimum of once every 2 weeks; keep the meeting short. When meeting with individual teachers about specific students, plan to spend no more than

5 minutes per student. To keep everyone fresh, meetings should be no longer than 30 minutes.

Procedures for Initial Meeting with Individual or Groups of Teachers

1. *Review the strategy and link its use to regular classroom success.* Provide the regular class teachers with a copy of the strategy steps. Describe the strategy and discuss the types of regular classroom requirements the strategy is designed to target. Collaborate with the teachers to identify the tasks in their classrooms in which use of the strategy will promote success. You should also work with the teachers to identify those tasks in their classrooms in which use of the strategy would not be appropriate.

2. *Discuss the importance of generalization.* Many regular education teachers are unfamiliar with the concept of generalization, so it will be important for you to explain why generalization is critical to student success at meeting the demands of the course. During this explanation emphasize the importance of enabling students to become independent as well as enabling them to meet the demands of the classroom. Once the teacher recognizes the importance of generalization, discuss factors that facilitate generalization as well as the roles of the key agents in this process.

3. *Collaborate with teachers to establish teaching plans.* Once teachers seem to appreciate the need for participating in teaching the strategy, discuss specific things they can do. Work together to identify the different ways they can cue, prompt, and model use of the strategy in the classroom. Help them identify ways they can incorporate use of the strategy into their instruction and materials.

Procedures for Subsequent Meetings with Individual or Groups of Teachers

1. *Ask teachers to identify and discuss students experiencing the most success generalizing the strategy.* Discuss success stories together before dealing with problems; as a result, the tone of the meeting will likely be more positive. Often, we run out of time to discuss what is going right when we begin by trying to solve problems.

2. *Discuss those students experiencing difficulty generalizing the strategy.*

- Discuss, in as specific terms as possible, assignments with which an individual student is experiencing success as well as those causing the student difficulty. Sometimes we have a tendency to discuss problems in general terms that provide little useful problem-solving information. Focus on specific tasks or behaviors. For example, if the teacher says, "Bill is doing pretty well," ask the teacher to elaborate on what assignments or tasks Bill is performing most successfully.

- Separate those tasks that relate to use of the strategy from those that do not. Often teachers experiencing frustration with a specific student will want to discuss a host of problems. To effectively address these, it is important for you to separate those related to generalization of the strategy from others that are not related to the strategy. This will enable you to focus on specific problems that have specific solutions.

- Discuss and develop plans for addressing problems students are experiencing that are not related to generalization of the strategy. In addition to discussing the students' use of the strategy in the teachers' classrooms, be sure to provide the teachers with opportunities to discuss problems not necessarily related to generalizing the strategy. Collaborate with teachers to generate potential solutions to these problems. Convert these ideas into specific action plans.

- Clarify the problems related to generalization of the strategy. Once you have focused the teacher's attention on problems with generalizing the strategy, clarify these by paraphrasing them back to the teacher.

- Review already developed plans for facilitating generalization. Before generating new plans for teaching, you should review the plans previously identified to determine whether the regular class teacher implemented them, and if so, what went wrong.

- Discuss and establish a plan for what you can do in your support class to promote use of the strategy in these teachers' classrooms. You may find that regular education teachers are more willing to engage support strategy teaching if you identify what you plan to do in *your* classroom to help them.

TROUBLESHOOTING

You may occasionally experience situations in which teachers with whom you are meeting do not seem interested in discussing shared teaching or students' progress with the strategy. If these are teachers who have previously been interested in discussing this topic, chances are that crises have arisen that require immediate attention. In these cases, first help the teachers address the "crisis" problems.

Another possibility is that the teachers may not clearly understand the purpose of the meeting or not be motivated to support the students' strategy use. If such a circumstance arises, consider using the following procedure: Suggest to the teachers that these meetings can be used for multiple purposes, and then encourage them to clarify their goals for the meetings (e.g., what they hope to accomplish, what types of information they would like to discuss, preferred ways to structure the meeting). Giving the teachers choices about topics can be an effective way to encourage them to discuss their preferences. Once the teachers have expressed goals for the meeting, ask them to identify goals they hope to accomplish as a result of meeting with you. Be sure to clarify your own goals as part of this process. Once you have clarified these goals, be sure you address them.

Teaching for Strategy Use in Regular Education Classes

GOAL: For regular education teachers to effectively use teaching procedures that promote use of a strategy in their classrooms.

ORIENTATION FOR THE REGULAR EDUCATION TEACHER

Students will often master a new learning strategy but then fail to use it at appropriate times in your classroom. Some students do not recognize these situations as opportunities to use the strategy, and some may know how to perform the strategy but not be sure as to how it can be applied to your course requirements. Others may lack sufficient motivation or be content to use less effective strategies. If you have students who have been learning specific learning strategies in support class settings, there are a number of relatively simple teaching techniques you can use to promote their use of the strategy in your classroom. These techniques also are effective for promoting use of specific strategies you may have been teaching. These instructional techniques focus on integrating cues, prompts, modeling, reinforcement, and feedback into your daily instruction and teaching materials. They are explained below.

Provide cues to use the strategy. For many students a simple reminder to use the strategy just before appropriate times can be sufficient. Both verbal cues (e.g., "This is a good time to use the DEFENDS Writing Strategy") and written cues (e.g., writing the name of the strategy on the board, adding the suggestion to use a strategy to directions on a study sheet) are effective. These cues can be provided discretely to individual students or to the whole class if they are familiar with the strategy.

Prompt use of the strategy. For some students you may need to provide more than simple reminders to use the strategy; you may need to prompt them to perform specific steps of the strategy. For example, if students are beginning a writing task that involves use of the DEFENDS Writing Strategy, you might need to structure prompts to ensure they perform prewriting activities before writing their essays. You might say something such as:

> *I want you to choose a political news story that happened this week that you think was important and write a short essay. Use DEFENDS. First, you will think ahead and organize your thoughts. Complete the organizer form and show it to me before writing the first draft of your essay.*

Model the strategy. You will find that many students will benefit from your modeling use of the strategy to meet the different demands in your classroom. Your modeling the strategy will make clear to students that you understand and value it. If you are promoting generalization of the FIRST-Letter Mnemonic Strategy, for example, you may model how they can memorize information in preparation for taking one of your tests or when organizing information for an oral report.

Provide reinforcement for using the strategy. One of the most important things you can do to promote generalization of a strategy is to reinforce students for using it. Students are responsive to simple verbal or written reinforcing comments. For example, a reinforcing verbal comment might be:

> *I noticed you seemed to be using the Paraphrasing Strategy to answer these questions. That was smart.*

An example of a written comment that might be written on the top of a student's paper:

> *Used DEFENDS. Great job!*

A few students may initially need more tangible reinforcers to help motivate them to use the strategy in your class. Examples include awarding extra credit or bonus points any time the student uses the strategy. For use of strategies that produce permanent products (e.g., written essays, class notes, written answers to study guide questions), you might consider giving two grades: one that reflects what you normally evaluate (e.g., whether the students included the correct information) and another for how well the student used the strategy to produce the product, regardless of accuracy.

You may ask your students who learned the strategy in another setting to share it with the other students in your class. Having them teach the strategy to another student can be reinforcing.

Provide feedback regarding how well they used the strategy. Not to be confused with reinforcement, providing effective feedback is also an important way to enhance students' use of the strategy in your classroom (feedback *can* be a form of reinforcement but is not always). Try to provide feedback in two areas. First, let students know how well they are recognizing opportunities to use the strategy. To do this, review the activities used during the content lesson and discuss opportunities students had to use the strategy, as well as whether they responded strategically to those instances. For example, if, during a civics lesson, you and your students were reading passages from the textbook and then discussing them, they could have used the Paraphrasing Strategy to offer main ideas and relevant details from each passage. You should provide feedback regarding whether they are realizing that paraphrasing can be used during this activity.

Second, provide students with explicit feedback regarding how well they are performing the strategy to meet your classroom demands. Feedback should include a focus on the parts of the strategy students are performing well (e.g., "You seem to be consistently using the organizer form as a prewriting activity"). Corrective feedback should also focus on error types (e.g., "You seem to be having a lot of difficulty with the part of the writing strategy that involves finding and correcting spelling errors") rather than on merely noting specific errors (e.g., "Look here, you misspelled these words").

Integrate strategy use with daily instruction and materials. Ideally, the academic environment should be such that using the strategy is part of the routine set of activities and requirements in your classroom. By integrating use of the strategy into your daily activities and assignments, you are sending the important message that students are encouraged, and indeed expected, to use the strategy.

There are two primary ways to integrate use of the strategy into daily instruction and materials. First, provide explicit instructions to use the strategy whenever appropriate. For example, instead of a study guide question from an American history class reading (e.g., "Why did the patriots almost disband their army at Valley Forge?"), the question can be reworded to provide explicit instructions to use the strategy to answer the question (e.g., "Use DEFENDS to explain why the American patriots almost disbanded their army at Valley Forge"). For another example, instead of having a student read aloud a specific passage from a text and then respond to one of your questions about the content of that passage, ask the student to use the Paraphrasing Strategy to paraphrase the main idea of the passage.

Second, use of a strategy can be more subtly integrated into instruction by your use of it when teaching the content. For example, use of an organizer form can be integrated into your health class lecture. Instead of using an overhead projector to display a traditional outline of your notes on the components of a healthy diet, display the same information using the organizer form. As a second example, use of the Paraphrasing Strategy can be routinely integrated into your instruction by frequently modeling the use of aspects of the strategy while alerting students that you are doing so; then have them practice using the strategy. For example:

> Let's take a look at this map of Europe in 1941. I'm going to paraphrase this map to tell the main idea and significant details. Let's see. The gray areas show the countries occupied by the Axis powers. I notice that most of Europe is gray, except for . . . Switzerland, England, and Spain. Let's see. Switzerland and Spain are colored differently from England; they were neutral. To paraphrase this, I need to tell the main idea and important details. Okay, here's the paraphrase: The main idea of this map is that the Axis powers had almost conquered all of Europe in 1941. Two details are that only three countries were not occupied by the Axis powers, and England was the only one who was not neutral. Looks like England was all by itself in the war against the Axis in 1941. So I've paraphrased the main idea and details of this map.

Let's look at the map on the next page. It depicts Europe at the end of World War II. Study it a moment to come up with a good paraphrase of it. I'm going to call on one of you to tell the main idea and significant details of that map in a minute.

WORKING RELATIONSHIP BETWEEN THE REGULAR EDUCATION TEACHER AND THE SUPPORT TEACHER

If students have been learning the strategy in a support class setting and you are trying to support this effort by promoting its generalization in your classroom, keep the support teacher informed about how well these students are using the strategy to meet the demands of your classroom. There are several things to keep in mind, as discussed below.

Your primary role is to teach the content of your courses, not to teach the strategies; the support teacher's role is to teach the strategies, not to provide tutoring in the content of your course. Neither is the "exclusive domain" of one teacher, however. You can enhance students' success in your classroom by promoting generalization of the strategies using the procedures described above. The support teacher can enhance students' success in your classroom by showing students how they can use the strategy to meet your class requirements and coaching them as they learn to do so. Teachers who do not regard their role as to teach all aspects of learning (i.e., content and the processes of learning) are naive about how learning occurs. For an excellent discussion on this topic, read Jones, Palincsar, Ogle, and Carr (1987).

Help support teachers understand the various requirements and demands of your class. If support teachers have a clear understanding of what students must do to be successful in your class, they will be in a better position to help select the best strategies to teach your students.

Meet with support teachers periodically as strategies are being learned and after they have been mastered by the students. You need to be informed about what strategies the students are learning and about their progress toward mastery. You will be in a better position to know what to expect from your students and may even need to raise your expectations as the strategies are mastered. By regularly communicating with support teachers, you will also be in a better position to know when to begin using supportive teaching procedures to promote generalization of the strategies. In addition, you will be better able to keep support teachers informed with regard to how well the students are using the strategies in your classroom.

Caution: You should be aware that there is a possibility that students can be inadvertently punished for attempting to generalize the strategy in your class. This can occur when you have a set of explicit expectations regarding how students are to perform a task that is not consistent with the behaviors associated with performing the strategy. For example, if you are a language arts teacher, you may want your students to follow a very explicit procedure when writing a book report. This procedure may be quite different from that associated with the DEFENDS Writing Strategy. Some students, thinking it would be a good time to use the DEFENDS strategy might use it and produce a well-organized essay about the book, but receive a low grade from you for not using the book report format you wanted used. If you foresee the potential for this type of trouble in upcoming assignments, alert students not to use the strategy if you do not want them to (but first, seriously question why you do not want them to use an effective learning technique).

PREPARATION

1. *Integrate cues for strategy use into printed instructional materials.* Look over the printed instructional materials used in an upcoming lesson (e.g., study guides, test questions, end-of-the-chapter questions) and analyze them to determine whether the instructions and/or specific questions can be modified to include explicit cues to use a strategy. Rewrite the appropriate items. Remember that students who are well on their way to strategy mastery or generalization will not need explicit cues such as "use the _____ strategy here."

2. *Design instructional activities that require use of specific learning strategies.* If you plan to integrate use of the strategy into your content instruction, you will need to design activities in which students will be able to use the learning strategy. If the strategy can be performed quickly, you can consider including multiple opportunities to use the strategy in a single lesson. If, however, the strategy requires several minutes or longer blocks of time to perform (e.g., the DEFENDS Writing Strategy), then one of these activities every few days may be more manageable.

3. *Design opportunities to model use of the strategy when providing instruction and then prompt students to perform the strategy.* Analyze the instructional objectives for the upcoming lesson and the activities you intend to use. Decide which activities can be modified to include strategy use.

TIME CONSIDERATIONS

Although use of the cooperative teaching procedures may seem like they require a great deal of extra time, they generally do not. Cueing students requires 2 to 3 seconds. Prompting, modeling, and providing reinforcement and feedback usually require only a few minutes, and the lesson is being accomplished as they are done.

The amount of time required to integrate use of the strategy with content instruction is negligible. You will be using the amount of time routinely used when teaching a content lesson. The difference is in the orientation of the activity. Now a greater emphasis is on using the best strategy when performing the activity. Normally, you would be providing students with feedback with regard to how well they performed the activity. Here, you'll be providing feedback that is simply more explicit—how well they used the best strategy when performing the activity.

PROCEDURES

1. *Determine opportunities for integrating use of the strategy into your teaching.* Use of some strategies can be readily integrated into your teaching. For example, you can integrate use of the Paraphrasing Strategy by modeling use of the strategy with specific passages from your textbook. Reflect on how you plan to present the content to students and determine when, if appropriate, you can integrate use of the strategy when teaching the content. Determine how you will alert the students to the fact that you are using the strategy.

2. *Analyze previously used instructional activities, assignments, and test questions to determine which can be adapted so that they are conducive to strategy use; design new activities, assignments, and test questions if necessary or appropriate.* When planning activities, assignments, and so on, which involve use of the new strategy, determine how you will use written and/or verbal cues to signal students to use the strategy (since you hope that students will eventually learn to independently recognize appropriate opportunities to use the strategy, you should not cue them to do so at every opportunity).

3. *Monitor students' use of the strategy. Monitor how well students use the strategy when given specific cues.* If students are not effectively performing the strategy, provide prompts to help them remember the strategy steps; model specific aspects of the strategy as necessary. Also, monitor how well students are recognizing opportunities for using the strategy when not given specific cues for its use, as well as how well they are performing the strategy under these circumstances. If students are independently recognizing opportunities for using the strategy, provide them with positive feedback and reinforcement for doing so. If students are not recognizing appropriate opportunities, review the characteristics of situations in which the strategy can be used. Also review with students their goals for generalizing the strategy.

4. *Communicate with the support teacher about how well students are performing the strategy as well as how well they are independently recognizing opportunities for its use.* If students originally learned the new strategy in a support class setting, periodically meet with the support teacher to discuss how well they are doing with regard to using the strategy to meet your class demands (about once every 1 to 2 weeks). The support teacher can provide the students with additional strategy instruction and support if needed.

INSTRUCTIONAL DECISIONS

How often should I provide students with activities that involve use of the strategy? Ideally, the more opportunities students have to perform the strategy to meet the demands of your classroom, the more effective they will become at both using the strategy and independently recognizing opportunities to use it. The frequency with which you provide these opportunities should, therefore, be as often as possible. Students should be provided daily opportunities to perform those strategies that can be performed relatively quickly (e.g., the Paraphrasing Strategy). Opportunities should be provided as often as possible to utilize strategies that require more extensive time to perform (e.g., the DEFENDS Writing Strategy).

TROUBLESHOOTING

If students are consistently failing to respond to explicit cues to use the strategy, the following techniques may help:

- Provide prompts to remind them of the strategy steps; model use of the steps if necessary.

- Pair a student who is failing to respond to cues with a student who readily responds. Ask the peer-tutor to help the student perform the strategy.

- Consider designing activities that involve less difficult materials until the student is more competent with the strategy. Students may be able to perform the strategy with less difficult materials. For example, they may be able to use the Paraphrasing Strategy when reading some textbooks written at an easier level, but not able to use it when reading more difficult texts. Or students may be able to use the DEFENDS Strategy when writing about topics that are generally familiar to them (e.g., a current news event) but unable to use it when writing about unfamiliar topics (e.g., the basic tenets of socialism).

- If the student originally learned the strategy in a support class setting, alert the support teacher that that student is unable to use the strategy, even when cued to do so, in your classroom. Additional instruction in the support class setting may be necessary.

If students are consistently failing to independently use the strategy, try doing the following:

- Provide prompts to alert them to an upcoming opportunity. For example, if a set of study guide questions might contain at least two different questions for which use of the DEFENDS Writing Strategy would be appropriate when answering the question, alert students to this fact. For example:

You have 15 study guide questions you will need to answer for home-work. You should use the DEFENDS Strategy with at least 2 of these. At the top of your page, write "2 Q's—DEFENDS" to help you remember that you should use it with 2 of these questions. I won't tell you which 2. You'll need to figure that out.

- Prompt students to analyze upcoming tasks to search for potential opportunities to use the strategy.

You have 15 study guide questions you will need to answer for home-work. You should use the DEFENDS Strategy with at least 2 of these. Look over these questions now. Try to figure out which 2 would be best for using the DEFENDS Strategy when writing your answer. Write "DEFENDS" next to those questions.

References

Adelman, H. S., & Taylor, L. (1983). *Learning disabilities in perspective.* Glenview, IL: Scott, Foresman.

Alley, G. R., & Deshler, D. D. (1979). *Teaching the learning disabled adolescent.* Denver, CO: Love.

Alley, G. R., Deshler, D. D., Clark, F., Schumaker, J. B., & Warner, M. (1983). Learning disabilities in adolescent and young adult populations: Research implications (Part II). *Focus on Exceptional Children, 15*(9), 1–14.

Anderson, R. C., & Armbruster, B. (1984). Content area textbooks. In R. C. Anderson, J. Osborn, & R. J. Tierney (Eds.), *Learning to read in American schools: Basal readers and content texts* (pp. 193–234). Hillsdale, NJ: Erlbaum.

Ausubel, D. P. (1960). The use of advance organizers in the learning and retention of meaningful verbal material. *Journal of Educational Psychology, 51,* 267–272.

Ausubel, D. P., Novak, J. D., & Hanesian, H. (1968). *Education psychology: A cognitive view* (2nd ed.). New York: Holt, Rinehart and Winston.

Bos, C. S., & Anders, P. L. (1990). Toward an interactive model: Teaching text based concepts to learning disabled students. In H. L. Swanson & B. Keogh (Eds.), *Learning Disabilities: Theoretical and research issues* (pp. 247–261). Hillsdale, NJ: Erlbaum.

Bransford, J., & Stein, B. S. (1984). *The ideal problem solver: A guide for improving thinking, learning, and creativity.* New York: Freeman.

Brown, A. L. (1978). Knowing when, where, and how to remember: A problem of metacognition. In R. Glaser (Ed.), *Advances in instructional psychology* (Vol. 1, pp. 77–165). Hillsdale, NJ: Erlbaum.

Brown, J. S., & Burton, R. R. (1978). Diagnostic models for procedural bugs in basic mathematical skills. *Cognitive Science, 2,* 155–192.

Bruer, J. T. (1993). *Schools for thought.* Cambridge, MA: MIT Press.

Crank, J., & Bulgren, J. A. (1993). Visual depictions as information organizers for enhancing achievement of students with learning disabilities. *Learning Disabilities Research & Practice, 8,* 140–147.

de Charms, R. (1976). *Enhancing motivation: A change in the classroom.* New York: Irvington.

Deshler, D. D., & Lenz, B. K. (1989). The strategies instructional approach. *International Journal of Disability, Development and Education, 36,* 203–224.

Deshler, D. D., & Schumaker, J. B. (1986). Learning strategies: An instructional alternative for low-achieving adolescents. *Exceptional Children, 52*(6), 483–590.

Deshler, D. D., Schumaker, J. B., & Lenz, B. K. (1984). Academic and cognitive interventions for LD adolescents: Part I. *Journal of Learning Disabilities, 17,* 108–117.

Deshler, D. D., Warner, M., Schumaker, J. B., & Alley, G. R. (1983). Learning strategies intervention model: Key components and current status. In J. D. McKinney & L. Feagans (Eds.), *Current topics in learning disabilities* (Vol. 1, pp. 245–283). Norwood, NJ: Ablex.

Ellis, E. (1985). *The effects of teaching learning disabled adolescents an executive strategy to facilitate self-generalization of task-specific strategies.* Unpublished doctoral dissertation, University of Kansas, Lawrence.

Ellis, E. (1986). The role of motivation and pedagogy on the generalization of cognitive strategy training. *Journal of Learning Disabilities, 19,* 66–70.

Ellis, E. (1994). *DEFENDS: A strategy for defending a position in writing.* Unpublished manuscript.

Ellis, E., Deshler, D. D., Lenz, B. K., Schumaker, J. B., & Clark, F. (1991). An instructional model for teaching learning strategies. *Focus on Exceptional Children, 23*(6), 1–24.

Ellis, E., Deshler, D. D., & Schumaker, J. B. (1989). Teaching adolescents with learning disabilities to generate and use task-specific strategies. *Journal of Learning Disabilities, 22,* 108–119.

Ellis, E., & Lenz, B. K. (1987). A component analysis of effective learning strategies for LD students. *Learning Disabilities Focus, 2,* 94–107.

Ellis, E., Lenz, B. K., & Sabornie, E. J. (1987a). Generalization and adaptation of learning strategies to natural environments: Part 1. Critical agents. *Remedial and Special Education, 8*(1), 6–20.

Ellis, E., Lenz, B. K., & Sabornie, E. J. (1987b). Generalization and adaptation of learning strategies to natural environments: Part 2. Research into practice. *Remedial and Special Education, 8*(2), 6–23.

Englert, C. S., Raphael, T. E., Anderson, L. M., Anthony, H. M., & Stevens, D. D. (1991). Making strategies and self-talk visible: Writing instruction in regular and special education classrooms. *American Educational Research Journal, 28*(2), 337–372.

Finch, A. J., Jr., & Spirito, A. (1980). Use of cognitive training to change cognitive processes. *Exceptional Education Quarterly: Teaching Exceptional Children to Use Cognitive Strategies, 1*(1), 31–39.

Gagné, R. M., & Brown, A. (1961). *The conditions of learning*. New York: Holt, Rinehart & Winston.

Howell, S. B. (1986). *A study of the effectiveness of TOWER—A theme writing strategy*. Unpublished master's thesis, University of Kansas, Lawrence.

Johnson, D. W., Johnson, R. T., & Holubec, E. (1988). *Cooperation in the classroom*. Edina, MN: Interaction Books.

Jones, B. F., Palincsar, A. M., Ogle, D., & Carr, E. G. (1987). *Strategic teaching and learning: Cognitive instruction in the content areas*. Alexandria, VA: Association for Supervision and Curriculum Development.

Kagan, S. (1992). The structural approach to cooperative learning. *Educational Leadership, 47*(4), 12–16.

Kea, C. D. (1987). *An analysis of critical teaching behaviors employed by teachers of students with mild handicaps*. Unpublished doctoral dissertation, University of Kansas, Lawrence.

Kline, F. (1989). *The development and validation of feedback routines for use in special education settings*. Unpublished doctoral dissertation, University of Kansas, Lawrence.

Lenz, B. K. (1982). *The effect of advance organizers on the learning and retention of learning disabled adolescents within the context of a cooperative planning model*. Unpublished doctoral dissertation, University of Kansas, Lawrence.

Lenz, B. K. (1983). Promoting active learning through effective instruction: Using advance organizers. *The Pointer, 27*(2), 11–13.

Lenz, B. K., Alley, G. R., & Schumaker, J. B. (1987). Activating the inactive learner: Advance organizers in the secondary content classroom. *Learning Disability Quarterly, 10*(1), 53–67.

Lenz, B. K., & Deshler, D. D. (1990). Principles of strategies instruction as the basis of effective preservice teacher education. *Teacher Education and Special Education, 13*(2), 82–95.

Lenz, B. K., Marrs, R. W., Schumaker, J. B., & Deshler, D. D. (1993). *The lesson organizer routine*. Lawrence, KS: Edge Enterprises.

Litch, B. C., & Kistner, J. A. (1986). Motivational problems of learning disabled children: Individual differences and their implications for treatment. In J. K. Torgesen & B. Y. L. Wong (Eds.), *Psychological and educational perspectives on learning disabilities* (pp. 225–255). New York: Academic Press.

Lloyd, J., & deBettencourt, L. (1982). *Academic strategy training: A manual for teachers*. Charlottesville: University of Virginia Learning Disabilities Institute.

Mayer, R. (1987). *Educational psychology: A cognitive approach*. Boston: Little, Brown.

Mehring, T. A., & Colson, S. E. (1990). Motivation and mildly handicapped learners. *Focus on Exceptional Children, 22*(5), 1–14.

Meichenbaum, D. M. (1977). *Cognitive behavior modification: An integrative approach*. New York: Plenum Press.

Meyer, B. F. J., Brandt, D., & Bluth, G. (1980). Use of top-level structure in text: Key to reading comprehension of ninth grade students. *Reading Research Quarterly, 16,* 72–103.

Nagel, D. R., Schumaker, J. B., & Deshler, D. D. (1986). *The learning strategies curriculum: The FIRST-Letter Mnemonic Strategy.* Lawrence, KS: Edge Enterprises.

Palincsar, A. M., & Brown, A. (1984). Reciprocal teaching of comprehensive fostering and comprehension monitoring strategies. *Cognition and Instruction, 1,* 117–175.

Pressley, M., Goodchild, F., Fleet, J., Zajchowski, R., & Evans, E. D. (1989). The challenges of classroom strategy instruction. *Elementary School Journal, 89,* 301–342.

Rademacher, J. (1993). *The collaborative development and validation of a classroom assignment routine to enhance the intrinsic motivation of students with learning disabilities.* Unpublished doctoral dissertation, University of Kansas, Lawrence.

Roehler, L. R., & Duffy, G. G. (1984). Direct explanation of comprehension progress. In G. G. Duffy, L. R. Roelher, & J. Mason (Eds.), *Comprehension instruction: Perspectives and suggestions.* New York: Longman.

Salomon, G. (1981). *Communication and education: Social and psychological interactions.* Beverly Hills, CA: Sage.

Scanlon, D. J., Duran, G. Z., Reyes, E. I., & Gallego, M. A. (1991). Interactive Semantic Mapping: An interactive approach to enhancing LD students' content area comprehension. *Learning Disabilities Research & Practice, 7,* 142–146.

Scanlon, D., Schumaker, J. B., & Deshler, D. D. (1994). Collaborative dialogues between teachers and researchers to create educational interventions: A case study. *Journal of Educational and Psychological Consultation, 5,* 69–76.

Scanlon, D., Schumaker, J. B., & Deshler, D. D. (1995). *The learning strategies curriculum: The listening and notetaking strategy.* Manuscript in preparation.

Schmidt, J. L. (1983). *The effects of four generalization conditions on learning disabled adolescents' written language performance in the regular classroom.* Unpublished doctoral dissertation, University of Kansas, Lawrence.

Schmidt, J. L., Deshler, D. D., Schumaker, J. B., & Alley, G. R. (1989). Effects of generalization instruction on the written language performance of adolescents with learning disabilities in the mainstream classroom. *Journal of Reading, Writing, and Learning Disabilities, 4,* 291–309.

Schumaker, J. B., Denton, P., & Deshler, D. D. (1984). *The learning strategies curriculum: The paraphrasing strategy.* Lawrence: University of Kansas, Institute for Research in Learning Disabilities.

Schumaker, J. B., & Deshler, D. D. (1992). Validation of learning strategy interventions for students with LD: Results of a programmatic research effort. In B. Y. L. Wong (Ed.), *Contemporary intervention research in learning disabilities: An international perspective* (pp. 22–46). New York: Springer-Verlag.

Schumaker, J. B., & Lyerla, K. (1991). *The Paragraph Writing Strategy.* Lawrence: University of Kansas.

Seabaugh, G. O., & Schumaker, J. B. (1981). *The effects of self-regulation training on the academic productivity of LD and NLD Adolescents* (Research Report No. 37). Lawrence: The University of Kansas Institute for Research in Learning Disabilities.

Simel, G. (1950). *Sociology of Georg Simel.* New York: Free Press.

Stone, C. A., & Wertsch, J. V. (1984). A social interactional analysis of learning disabilities remediation. *Journal of Learning Disabilities, 17*(4), 194–199.

Taylor, B. M., & Beach, R. W. (1984). The effects of text structure instruction on middle-grade students' comprehension and production of expository text. *Reading Research Quarterly, 19,* 134–146.

Torgesen, J. (1977). Memorization processes in reading-disabled children. *Journal of Educational Psychology, 79,* 571–578.

Vygotsky, L. S. (1978). *Mind and society: The development of higher psychological processes* (M. Cole, V. John-Steiner, S. Scribner, & E. Souberman, Eds.). Cambridge, MA: Harvard University Press.

Wong, B. Y. L. (1979). Increasing retention of main ideas through questioning strategies. *Learning Disability Quarterly, 2,* 42–47.

Wong, B. Y. L.(1985). Potential means of enhancing content skills acquisition in learning disabled adolescents. *Focus on Exceptional Children, 17,* 1–8.

Wong, B. Y. L. (1994). Instructional parameters promoting transfer of learned strategies in students with LD. *Learning Disability Quarterly, 17,* 110–120.

Wong, B. Y. L., & Sawatsky, D. (1984). Sentence elaboration and retention of good, average and poor readers. *Learning Disability Quarterly, 7*(3), 229–236.

Appendix A

Sources of Information on SIM Products

The following SIM materials are available from:

(Some of the materials may be purchased only in conjunction with participation in training)

Center for Research on Learning
3061 Dole Center
University of Kansas
Lawrence, KS 66045
(913) 864-4780

Enhancing Strategies Instruction: Critical Teaching Behaviors (video)
Making a Difference: From Those Who Know (video)
Modeling the FIRST-Letter Mnemonic Strategy (video)
Modeling the Sentence Writing Strategy (video)
Teaching Younger Students to Master Learning Strategies (video)
The Error Monitoring Strategy
The Paragraph Writing Strategy: Instructor's Manual
The Paraphrasing Strategy
The Sentence Writing Strategy: Instructor's Manual
The Visual Imagery Strategy
The Word Identification Strategy

The following SIM materials are available from:

(Some of the materials may be purchased only in conjunction with participation in training)

> **Edge Enterprises, Inc.**
> P.O. Box 1304
> Lawrence, KS 66044
> (913) 749-1473

Addition Facts 0 to 9
Collaborative Problem Solving
Division Facts 0 to 81
Helping Students Master Social Skills (video)
Keys to Success in Learning Strategy Instruction (video)
Keys to Success in Social Skills Instruction (video)
LINCS: A Starter Strategy™ for Vocabulary Learning
Multiplication Facts 0 to 81
Place Value: Discovering Tens & Ones
Sentence FUNdamentals™
SLANT: A Starter Strategy™ for Class Participation
Subtraction Facts 0 to 9
The Concept Anchoring Routine
The Concept Mastery Routine
The Education Planning Strategy
The FIRST-Letter Mnemonic Strategy
The Lesson Organizer Routine
The Paragraph Writing Strategy: Student Lessons
The Progress Program
The SCORE Skills: Social Skills for Cooperative Groups
The Self-Advocacy Strategy
The Sentence Writing Strategy: Student Lessons
The Teamwork Strategy
The Test-Taking Strategy
The Unit Organizer Routine

For information on SIM training:

> Training Facilitator
> Center for Research on Learning
> 3061 Dole Center
> University of Kansas
> Lawrence, KS 66045
> (913) 864-4780

Selected publications pertaining to SIM:

Deshler, D. D., & Lenz, B .K. (1989). The strategies instructional approach. *International Journal of Disability, Development and Education, 36,* 203–224.

Deshler, D. D., & Schumaker, J. B. (1988). An instructional model for teaching students how to learn. In J. L. Graden, E. Zins, & M. J. Curtis (Eds.), *Alternative educational delivery systems: Enhancing instructional options for all students* (pp. 391–411). Washington, DC: National Association of School Psychologists.

Deshler, D. D., Schumaker, J. B., & Lenz, B. K. (1984). Academic and cognitive interventions for LD adolescents: Part I. *Journal of Learning Disabilities, 17,* 108–117.

Deshler, D. D., & Schumaker, J. B., Lenz, B. K., & Ellis, E. S. (1984). Academic and cognitive interventions for LD adolescents: Part II. *Journal of Learning Disabilities, 17,* 170–187.

Deshler, D. D., Warner, M. W., Schumaker, J. B., & Alley, G. R. (1983). Learning strategies intervention model: Key components and current status. In J. D. McKinney & L. Feagans (Eds.), *Current topics in learning disabilities* (Vol. 1, pp. 245–283). Norwood, NJ: Ablex.

Ellis, E. S., & Lenz, B. K. (1987). A component analysis of effective learning strategies for LD students. *Learning Disabilities Focus, 2,* 94–107.

Ellis, E. S., Deshler, D. D., Lenz, B. K., Schumaker, J. B., & Clark, F. L. (1991). An instructional model for teaching learning strategies. *Focus on Exceptional Children, 23*(6), 1–24.

Lenz, B. K., Bulgren, J. A., & Hudson, P. (1990). Content enhancement: A model for promoting the acquisition of content by individuals with learning disabilities. In T. E. Scruggs & B. Y. L. Wong (Eds.), *Intervention research in learning disabilities* (pp. 122–165). New York: Springer-Verlag.

Platt, J. M., & Beech, M. (1994). The effectiveness of learning strategies in improving performance and increasing the independence of juvenile offenders with learning problems. *Journal of Correctional Education, 45*(1), 18–24.

Schumaker, J. B., Deshler, D. D., Alley, G. R., & Warner, M. W. (1983). Toward the development of an intervention model for learning disabled adolescents. *Exceptional Education Quarterly, 4,* 45–71.

Appendix B

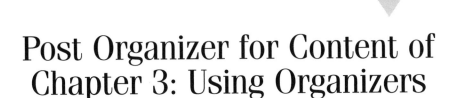

Post Organizer for Content of Chapter 3: Using Organizers

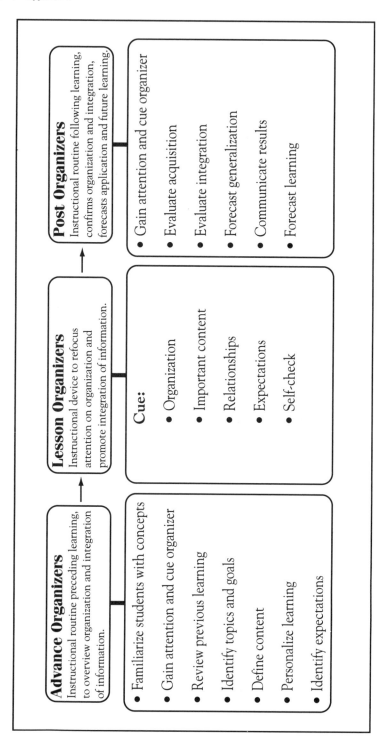

Advance Organizers
Instructional routine preceding learning, to overview organization and integration of information.

- Familiarize students with concepts
- Gain attention and cue organizer
- Review previous learning
- Identify topics and goals
- Define content
- Personalize learning
- Identify expectations

Lesson Organizers
Instructional device to refocus attention on organization and promote integration of information.

Cue:

- Organization
- Important content
- Relationships
- Expectations
- Self-check

Post Organizers
Instructional routine following learning, confirms organization and integration, forecasts application and future learning.

- Gain attention and cue organizer
- Evaluate acquisition
- Evaluate integration
- Forecast generalization
- Communicate results
- Forecast learning

NOTES

NOTES

NOTES

NOTES

NOTES

NOTES

NOTES

NOTES

NOTES

NOTES

NOTES

NOTES